The Way of the Dreamcatcher

Spirit Lessons with Robert Lax:
Poet, Peacemaker, Sage

Robert Lax (1915–2000)

The Way
of the Dreamcatcher

Spirit Lessons with Robert Lax:
Poet, Peacemaker, Sage

Steve Theodore Georgiou

NOVALIS

© 2002 Novalis, Saint Paul University, Ottawa, Canada

Cover design: Caroline Gagnon

Cover art: Painting of Robert Lax by Edward Rice, 1968,
courtesy of Chris Rice

Layout: Suzanne Latourelle, Caroline Gagnon and Francyne Petitclerc

Photographs: Unless otherwise noted, all photos are courtesy of the author.

Excerpt on p. 281 is from *Beautiful Losers*, by Leonard Cohen. Used by permission, McClelland & Stewart Ltd., *The Canadian Publishers*.

Business Office:
Novalis
49 Front Street East, 2nd Floor
Toronto, Ontario, Canada
M5E 1B3
Phone: 1-800-387-7164 or (416) 363-3303
Fax: 1-800-204-4140 or (416) 363-9409
E-mail: cservice@novalis.ca

National Library of Canada Cataloguing in Publication Data

Georgiou, Steve Theodore

The way of the dreamcatcher : spirit lessons with Robert Lax, poet,
peacemaker, sage

ISBN 2-89507-244-2

1. Lax, Robert—Interviews. 2. Poets, American—20th century—
Interviews. 3. Lax, Robert—Criticism and interpretation. I. Title.

PS3523.A9752Z6 2002   811'.54   C2002-901035-7

Printed in Canada.

We acknowledge the financial support of the Government of Canada through the Book Publishing Industry Development Program (BPIDP) for our publishing activities.

10 9 8 7 6 5 4 3 2 1   2010 2009 2008 2007 2006 2005 2004 2003 2002

To my father, Theodore,

(1926–1999)

who is dreaming with us

INTO THE DREAM

It is only after a pious journey to a distant region, in a strange land, a new country, that the meaning of the inner voice guiding our search can be revealed to us. And added to that strange and constant fact is another: that the person who reveals the meaning of our mysterious inner voyage must himself be a stranger...

—Heinrich Zimmer, *Myths and Symbols in Indian Art and Civilization*, edited by Joseph Campbell

A true teacher has no need to call the seeker; he lets the disciple come.

—Buddhist proverb

If you find a man who is constant, awake to the inner light, learned, long suffering, endowed with devotion, a noble man – follow this good and great man even as the moon follows the path of the stars.

—*The Dhammapada* 15.208, translated by Juan Mascaro

A teacher for a day is like a parent for a lifetime.

—Chinese proverb

The teacher, therefore, is the man who does all that he does sufficiently, and the core of his teaching is this, that he lets his disciple take part in his life and thus grasp the mystery of the action.

—Martin Buber, *The Origin and Meaning of Hasidism*, translated and edited by Maurice Friedman

An experience that is true will be true throughout life. Its character is personal and also universal. It is practical and also symbolic… An experience seems to be in "one man" but is meant for "Everyman."

—Meg Maxwell and Verina Tschudin, *Seeing the Invisible: Modern Religious and Other Transcendent Experiences*

And your young man shall see visions,
and your old men shall dream dreams...

—Acts 1.17

An old man and a child would walk together
and the old man be led on his path
and the child left thinking...

—John Keats

To give oneself, body, speech, and heart, to the cause of
Holy Truth is the best and highest occupation ...
Ever transient is this world of ours,
all things change and pass away;
For a distant journey even now prepare.

—Last Testamentary Teachings of the Guru
Phadama Sangay

The Tibetan Book of the Great Liberation, edited by
Evans-Wentz

CONTENTS

ACKNOWLEDGMENTS

My meetings with the late Robert Lax on the remote Greek island of Patmos have been both a spiritual and creative odyssey. I remain infinitely grateful for his friendship and for his help in creating this book. As many others have said, Lax was a born teacher and poet, and I feel blessed to have met him in the summer of 1993, a meeting which came to be the first of many. With his encouragement, I often revisited this wizard-like hermit and sage – a "Dreamcatcher" whose wisdom and love helped me to apprehend and cultivate my gifts. Through Lax, my spiritual and artistic vision was restored and amplified; a fresh desire to live joyfully and embrace the cosmos with *agape* was renewed in me. Small wonder that towards the end of his life, an actual dreamcatcher – that popular Native American creation meant to insure peaceful, lucid dreaming – hung from the ceiling lantern of his hermitage. Indeed, many of our last talks took place beneath the ringed and feathered talisman. The colourful, protective creation seemed to grace our meetings, adding a special harmony and wonder to them.

In late fall of 1999, shortly before Robert's passing, I conducted a series of interviews with the sage-poet having to do with his life, work, artistic interests, and spiritual beliefs. Together with material gathered from past encounters and conversations, these thematic exchanges form the basis of this book. To a great degree, this inspirational project is a way of saying "thank you" to Robert; it is a creative and soul-centred summation of the teacher–student relationship and free-flowing friendship that we shared over the years.

In writing this book, I would like to thank Robert's many friends on Patmos whose sincere kindness aptly prepared me for my visits with Bob. Special thanks goes to Niko and Ritsa Eliou, Anastasia Grillis, Sophia and the late Yianni Kamitsi, Panteli and Caliopi Kleudis, and the Archimandrite Efthimiou Koutsanelos, Superior of the Holy Cave of St. John the Divine.

My gratitude also extends to the many writers, artists, and spirit-seekers whom I have met on Patmos, all of whom considered Robert to have been a great source of inspiration and wisdom. I am sure each has their own stories to tell about the *aghios peoitis*, or "holy poet," as Robert was sometimes referred to by the islanders. For Lax shared his life and charity with all who came his way. As Thomas Merton said of his beloved friend, "I think he has told what he has to say to many people..." (*The Seven Storey Mountain*, 237).

In creating this work, I thank Michael Morris, O.P., for his constant encouragement and help in integrating its contents into my doctoral studies at the Graduate Theological Union at Berkeley, California, where I am completing my degree in the Arts and Religion program. My gratitude also goes to the following professors at the Graduate Theological Union, Berkeley: Doug Adams, Luke Buckles, O.P., Jane Dillenberger, Reindert Falkenburg, and William Short, O.F.M. I also thank Jacob Needleman, Professor of Philosophy and World Religions at San Francisco State University, for his continual inspiration and advice.

Among Robert's many friends in the States, I am especially grateful to Robert Giroux of Farrar, Straus, and Giroux, Brother Patrick Hart of the Abbey of Gethsemani in Kentucky, and Jonathan Montaldo, former Director of the Thomas Merton Center in Louisville, Kentucky, for their direction and support along the path leading to publication. Special thanks goes to Robert's immediate family, Marcia and Jack Kelley and Connie Brothers, for their good wishes and encouragement; Kevin Burns, Commissioning Editor of Novalis, whose unflagging faith in this project helped bring the book to light; Jim Forest, founder of the Orthodox Peace Fellowship, for his cheerful inspiration; and Paul Spaeth, Curator of the Lax Archives at St. Bonaventure University, for his friendship and forthright assistance in things Laxian. Gratitude also goes to Harriet Hope and Susannah Malarkey of the Santa Sabina Center in San Rafael, California, who have kept alive the spirit of Lax and his dear friend, Thomas Merton, in their monthly "Merton Reflection Evenings." And I remain very grateful to my late father, Theodore, my mother, Anastasia, and my sister, Maria, who, after journeying with me to Patmos in 1997, at last met Bob, and saw first-hand why I kept on returning to the isle. Their support has been a great comfort.

Finally, there is one person I would like to thank but most likely never will, because his identity remains a mystery. He is the young man who brought Lax to my attention a few days after my first arrival on Patmos. This incident is described in its entirety later in the book, but to this day, I keep on wondering about that individual who approached me one night while I sat by the waterfront. He pointed towards the mountain of Kastelli and said that I should go up in that direction and find a sage named "Pax." Of course, he had the name wrong, but, in a strange way, it was right, because in Latin, "Pax" denotes *peace*. And this is what Robert has given me and has gently bestowed unto all who have had the good fortune to meet him. He was a Peacemaker, a Spirit-King who quietly, unselfconsciously gave those he met the strength to grow and actualize their dreams. I hope that through this book, his wisdom, power, wit, and compassion will extend to many more people, all of whom Robert continues to infinitely love.

Look far back,
look infinitely on.
Penetrate, do not appraise.
Behold all things
with the innocence of light.
Laugh when you meet a stranger;
let your glances flash together
like water in sunlight.

Robert Lax,
adapted from
Circus of the Sun

TO THE READER

It was a great experience for me to have read this heart-warming collection of exchanges between the late Robert Lax and his friend Steve Georgiou, especially since I had the rare privilege of meeting Lax in his hermitage on the Greek island of Patmos several years ago. My visit with Lax – the noted American poet, sage and lifelong friend of Thomas Merton – was both a profound and moving experience, and I came to understand why Merton said of him, "He had a kind of inborn direction to the living God" (The Seven Storey Mountain, 180–181).

In reading *The Way of the Dreamcatcher*, I was delightfully transported back to my blessed encounter with the "Poet of Patmos." His radiant wisdom and humour come to life in these timeless conversations. In essence, this valuable book gives everyone the chance to journey to the holy and enchanted isle of the Apocalypse and visit Lax in his rustic hilltop hermitage overlooking the Aegean Sea. This warm, inspiring text allows the reader to learn and laugh with a man numerous authors have affectionately termed "a saint."

Lax and Georgiou are truly kindred spirits. They seem to understand one another intuitively and breathe forth wonderful insights into the questions that confront us all. We find in this collection the spirited queries of a younger artist and scholar who approaches Lax for words of wisdom and insight into the deepest meanings of life, and we are gifted with the moving responses of a poet and sage of great distinction, though not widely enough known or appreciated.

Amazingly, Georgiou has managed to give us a portrait of Lax that is at once historical, personal, and intimate while, at the same, cosmic in its ramifications. This wise man's relationship to God and his fellow humans bears significance for us all. In his graced existence, the gentle poet enriched so many lives simply through his calm, peaceful and incredibly giving nature. A radiant bearer of bliss, Robert Lax wholly merits the title Georgiou has given his friend and teacher: *Dreamcatcher*. May this work's wisdom, creativity, playful spirit, and manifold message of love deeply and happily influence many readers.

Brother Patrick Hart, O.C.S.O
Last Secretary to Thomas Merton
General Editor of the Merton Journals
Abbey of Gethsemani
June, 2001

PATMOS

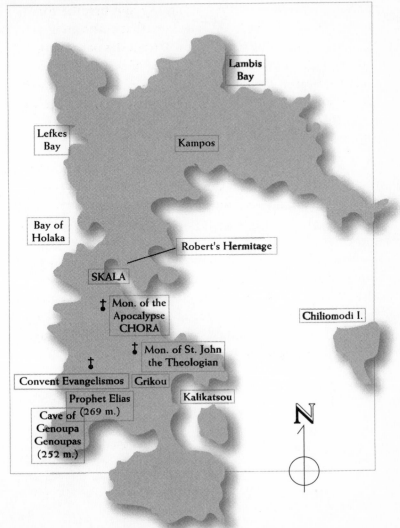

Lambis
Bay

Lefkes
Bay

Kampos

Bay of
Holaka

Robert's Hermitage

SKALA

† Mon. of the
Apocalypse
CHORA

† Mon. of St. John
the Theologian

Convent Evangelismos | Grikou

Prophet Elias
(269 m.)

Kalikatsou

Cave of
Genoupa
Genoupas
(252 m.)

Chiliomodi I.

N

PROLOGUE

Spirit Bearer

Robert Lax (1915–2000), one of the foremost minimalist poets of the late twentieth century and the best friend of the renowned Trappist monk Thomas Merton, lived on the remote Greek islands of Kalymnos and Patmos for nearly forty years. Prior to his departure from the United States in 1964, he was highly instrumental in Merton's spiritual growth – Merton himself hailed Lax as his "spiritual superior."

> Lax was born with the deepest sense of who God was…. He was much wiser than I, and he had clearer vision, and was, in fact, corresponding much more truly to the grace of God than I, and he had seen what was the one important thing. I think he has told what he has to say to many people besides myself, but certainly his was one of the many voices through which the insistent

Spirit of God was determined to teach me the way
I had to travel…. To sum it up, even people who
had always thought he was "too impractical" have
always tended to venerate him….[1]

Merton converted to Catholicism and entered the
Monastery of Our Lady of Gethsemani in Kentucky; Lax,
born a Jew, also converted to Catholicism and eventually
chose the solitary life of a poet and hermit. Through a
mystical sign he received in Marseille, he selected Patmos,
the holy isle of St. John's Revelation, as his literary and
spiritual workshop. Although in his lifetime he was not
well known in the United States, in Europe he enjoyed a
quiet reputation as a man of letters, a friend of the arts,
and a sage.

It remains strange why Lax and his striking, original
work – primarily focusing on his spiritual relationships
with people, places, and ideas – have in many ways
escaped popular attention. Arts critic Richard Kostelanetz,
writing in *The New York Times Review of Books*, said of Lax,
"He is among America's greatest experimental poets, a true
minimalist who can weave awesome poems from
remarkably few words…. Lax remains the last
unacknowledged – and, alas, uncollected – major poet of
his post-60 generation."[2] The literary critic R.C. Kenedy
of the Victoria and Albert Museum remarked, "In my
opinion, *Circus of the Sun* (one of Lax's early and perhaps
most famous titles), is, in all probability, the finest volume

of poems published by an English speaking poet of the generation which comes in T.S. Eliot's wake."[3]

For all of Lax's obscurity, his name is familiar to much of the world, especially readers of theology. He appears throughout Thomas Merton's *The Seven Storey Mountain*, as both his closest friend and spirit colleague. In this famous book which has been compared to Augustine's *Confessions*, Merton, the most influential proponent of monasticism in America and perhaps the greatest contemporary religious writer and pioneer in interfaith dialogue, describes his companion as he appeared at about 25. Significantly, the identical portrayal well depicted Lax even into his last years.

> He was a kind of Hamlet and Elias. A potential prophet, but without rage. A king, but a Jew too. A mind full of tremendous and subtle intuitions, and every day he found less and less to say about them, and resigned himself to being inarticulate. In his hesitations, though without embarrassment or nervousness at all, he would often curl his long legs all around a chair, in seven different ways, while he was trying to find out a word with which to begin. He talked best sitting on the floor.

> And the secret of his constant solidity I think has always been a kind of natural, instinctive spirituality, a kind of inborn direction to the living God. Lax has always been afraid he was in a blind

25

alley, and half aware that, after all, it might not be a blind alley, but God, infinity.

He had a mind naturally disposed from the very cradle to a kind of affinity for Job and St. John of the Cross. And I now know that he was born so much of a contemplative that he will probably never be able to find out how much.... [4]

Lax was crucial to Merton's spiritual evolution. It was Lax's "instinctive spirituality" which had urged the young Merton to follow his bliss and embrace God with the whole of his being. In essence, Lax urged Merton to become what every ardent lover of God is capable of becoming – a *saint*.

Lax suddenly turned around and asked me a question.

"What do you want to be, anyway?"

I could not say, "I want to be Thomas Merton the well-known writer." So I put the thing on the spiritual plane, where I knew it belonged, and said:

"I don't know; I guess what I want to be is a good Catholic."

"What do you mean, you want to be a good Catholic?"

The explanation I gave was lame enough, and expressed my confusion, and betrayed how little I had really thought about it all.

Lax did not accept it.

"What you should say" – he told me – "what you should say is that you want to be a saint."

A saint! The thought struck me as a little weird. I said:

"How do you expect me to be a saint?"

"By wanting to," said Lax simply.

"I can't be saint," I said. "I can't be a saint..."

But Lax said: "No. All that is necessary to be a saint is to want to be one. Don't you believe that God will make you what He created you to be, if you consent to let Him do it? All you have to do is desire it."[5]

Since their student days at Columbia University, Lax's insight and overarching wisdom had always made sense to Merton. Over the years, his calm disposition and quiet gentleness had worked its way into his friend's mind and heart. Ultimately, Lax inspired Merton to consistently aim high in the life of grace.

Merton was not alone in perceiving Lax's natural ability to illumine and inspire. Mark Van Doren, the distinguished English professor and poet at Columbia University who had taught both Lax and Merton, also discerned how Lax was graced with a kind of inherent, free flowing and affirming wisdom that stemmed from "the irrepressible love of the world and all things in it."[6] And Catherine de Hueck Doherty, a Russian baroness who had founded "Friendship House," a Catholic settlement for the poor in Harlem where both Lax and Merton had volunteered their services, said of Lax:

> We talked easily. I liked him. He was young, and had the long, gentle face of a poet, a dreamer, a student.... In the course of our slow, random, yet friendly conversation, he told me he was a poet, wrote for the *New Yorker*, and was a Jew, an Orthodox Jew.... He was filled with charity, and he warmed with his love our little Madonna flat in Harlem. He was worth listening to. We all prayed the official evening prayer of the Church. Somehow he made the Psalms of David come alive for us. He recited them with so much fervor.... *Caritas*, otherwise known as Love, spoke loudly in his every gesture. It shone in his face and spoke through his words.... There were many incidents with this son of Israel, but I'm afraid it would take a whole book. He is the kind of man about whom someday books may be written.[7]

Interestingly, it was Lax's association with Friendship House which helped to catalyze his baptism at the age of 28.

Thus at about the same time that Merton had entered a Trappist monastery, Lax had embraced Catholicism.

Laughing Buddha

Prior to 2000, Robert Lax was still to be seen walking the streets of Skala, the harbour town of Patmos. Toward evening he usually left his little hermitage overlooking the bay and descended the winding hill of Kastelli. With a long wooden staff in one hand and a blue denim bag in the other, he quietly made his way toward the fishing boats where he strolled, meditated, and talked to numerous locals eager to exchange a few words. On his return trip, he stopped at various shops to buy food for his many cats and also purchased yogurt and other standard health provisions which constituted his daily fare.

Lax cut a memorable figure. Tall, lean, and sporting a white beard that hinted of righteousness, he could not help but command attention, even though his humble, unassuming presence indicated quite the contrary. Wearing blue jeans, a white canvas jacket, and a broad-brimmed straw hat, he easily blended into his rustic surroundings and could be mistaken for an elderly fisherman, a patriarch of the Aegean. At the same time, his long, ascetic face imparted an almost medieval quality, as though he were a cross between King Arthur and Moses.

And if one were to suggest a more recent and perhaps more popular likeness, Lax looked much like the ancient knight featured in the final scene of the film *Indiana Jones and the Last Crusade*, the faithful warrior who swore an oath to guard the Holy Grail indefinitely; in many ways, Lax took on the same noble attributes.

When Lax greeted people, he looked at them with a kind of happy awe, as if hailing a company of saints. He addressed his audience with kindness and focused on them completely, carefully, honestly, and with genuine love. His gentle blue eyes, deep set and empathetic, sparkled and became liquid portals of grace. Sparks would fly, and those who left him broke into warm and carefree smiles, having been uplifted by an energy born of a lifetime of theocentric living. The radiant poet had a way of reminding people that they were beloved children of God, cherished participants in a holy mystery. Small wonder why many who met Lax believed him to be a saint. Jack Kerouac, an early friend of Lax, aptly referred to him as "Laughing Buddha."[8]

This "positive energy transmission" remained much in keeping with Lax's intercommunal philosophy of life. People, empowered by God, were created to help one another. As Lax wrote, "We are beings charged with energy, exchanging charges throughout the day."[9] Certainly this interactive outlook may be traced to Lax's early studies of Jewish mysticism which embodied many elements of Hasidic teaching.

Everything wants to be hallowed, to be brought into the holy...everything wants to become sacrament.... Things seek us out on our paths; what comes to meet us on our way needs us for its way...everything wants to come to us, everything wants to come to God through us...let the hidden light of God shine forth.[10]

In a quiet, unpretentious way, Lax's "life of charity" demonstrated how this may be done. Even into his last years, the elderly poet continued to inspire those who came to him from around the world. Many who visited Patmos did so in the hopes of meeting the noted writer and sage. Indeed, every summer, a small gathering of artists and students, mostly from Europe, visited Lax and simply by being in his company were inspired to become better people. Sometimes they met at the seaside Arion café in Skala or else walked with their "teacher" along the long concrete dock extending from the port city's shore.

As might be expected of a reclusive, dedicated contemplative, Lax did not talk much, nor did he desire manifold attention. Instead, he preferred to maintain a low profile and listened intently, using his own silence to draw ideas out of others, in this way helping his visitors find solutions to their own problems. It might be said that while Lax supplied the spiritual inspiration, those who sought him out oftentimes arrived at their own carefully thought-out answers. Like Plato and Confucius, Lax understood that students best profit from truths that they have self-discovered. But Lax's "silent way of instruction" demonstrated a mystical dimension as well. Essentially, the unassuming, soft-spoken poet thought it best to remain an "empty vessel" through which a greater power could work. Like the restraint and "empty space" of his verse, Lax minimized himself and became a living channel through which a type of higher wisdom flowed. Rather than focus attention on himself or on any fixed method of instruction, Lax hinted at something greater than human design, a divine force that incessantly sought to awaken people to a transcendent way of awareness and being. He only asked that people *relax* in order to sense God operating in themselves and the cosmos. However, when Lax did speak at length, his words were inestimable, because sooner or later his insights – oftentimes peppered with zany humour – came to have great personal meaning.[11]

The Dream Unfolds

In the summer of 1993, I visited Patmos and met Lax in a rather unusual manner. At that time, I had no knowledge of the eremitical poet, nor was I familiar with Thomas Merton, even though I had recently received my graduate degree in the Interdisciplinary Humanities and had begun to teach at various San Francisco colleges. However, one night, while I was in Skala watching an incoming ferry head into port, a young, thickly-bearded Greek waiting to board approached and we began a conversation.

"You are French? German?" he asked in halting English, simultaneously displaying the pointed curiosity for which the Greeks are famous.

"No, I'm American," I replied, and added that my roots were Greek, my grandparents having been born in Asia Minor and mainland Greece.

The young man smiled, sensing a camaraderie. "What is your work in America?"

"I'm a college teacher in California," I replied. "I teach about thought and art, and like to write."

"What do you write?"

"Poems, and scholarly things too."

"Do you believe in God?" he suddenly asked.

"Why, yes," I answered. "I'm Greek Orthodox, just as you may be. I follow the faith and study the Fathers."

A brief silence ensued. Then he said, "You know, there is an American writer living on Patmos. He likes art, philosophy. You should talk to him."

"Who is he?" I asked.

"A wise old poet in the hills," replied the youth, pointing to the mountain of Kastelli behind us. "His name is Pax."

"Pax?" I said. "That means *peace* in Latin!"

The young Greek appeared not to understand the significance of my remark. But within me, something began to stir, because the truth was that I had journeyed to Patmos to *find* peace, having experienced inner unrest, the cumulative result of family illness, work-related stress, and the end of a long-term relationship. The unusual name of the friendly sage-poet therefore seemed auspicious, and I began to wonder if he could indeed help me find solace.

To be sure, this "Pax" had chosen a most idyllic isle on which to live and write. For centuries Patmos had acquired a reputation for serenity and holiness. It was a refuge for spirit-seekers and wandering pilgrims. This "Jerusalem of the Aegean" especially owed its fame to St. John, author of the Book of Revelation. According to many theologians of the early Church, this same St. John was St. John the Disciple and Evangelist. Serving as the isle's protector and intercessor, he was termed the "Apostle of Love." Somehow it seemed both strange and appropriate that on an isle widely known for its holiness and tranquility, a poet named "Peace" resided.

"So will you go?" asked the young Greek. "Will you go to Pax?"

"But isn't it getting rather late?" I asked. "How can I go off and visit a man I don't even know?"

"Go, just go!" he insisted. "Take the road in back of the Arion café. It goes a long way. Go up, and you will find his house."

Before I could ask the youth anything more, he hurriedly picked up his bags and boarded the ferry. Though somewhat wary of his insistent manner, I concluded that he was being truthful, and took him up on the offer. As the ferry lights disappeared, I turned toward the direction I had been pointed in and began the long ascent leading to the poet's dwelling, asking for more precise directions along the way.

As I walked up the winding street, I looked back and could see the distant waterfront through the gaps between the houses facing the sea. The ferry boat bearing the young Greek who had directed me to "Pax" was quickly steaming through the island gates, its bellowing horn blasting a final farewell.

Sporadic lights illuminated the increasingly steep ascent. The clean whitewashed homes stood out of the darkness and guided me onward and upward through wide and narrow passages. The higher I rose, the fainter the sounds of Skala became. Only the occasional roar of a scooter or children's voices at play cut through the windy silence. Suddenly an old woman opened a door and tossed fish to an alley cat. We had startled each other, and together we laughed.

"Pou eineh o Pax?" I asked in Greek. "Where is Pax?"

Her bright eyes narrowed a bit. Then a hint of a smile flashed across her face.

"Thelies ton peiti?" she queried. "Do you want the poet?"

I nodded, and was told to continue up the long street, then make a right at the top. Lax lived in a small blue-white house situated towards the end of the road.

"Efcharisto" ("Thank you"), I said, as I turned to go.

"Yassoo!" ("Health be with you"), she softly exclaimed.

Health must certainly have been with the old poet. I was perspiring by the time I got to the end of the street and mounted a series of high stone steps. For a few moments I paused to catch my breath and saw the faraway lights of the great Monastery of St. John twinkling like stars.

All at once the walls had gotten narrower. With the help of a pocket flashlight, I carefully made my way along an irregular concrete pavement until I came to a clearing. Within moments, I found myself outside a small house that fit the description I was given.

It was about 9 p.m. I knocked on a frail wooden door, unaware that "the poet" vigilantly guarded his privacy and allowed few people up to his dwelling.

"Pax! Pax!" I shouted. "Are you there?"

For a few minutes I waited on the porch but heard nothing, only the wind winding its way through the heights of Kastelli. Thinking the poet to be out or asleep, I turned to go.

And then I heard a voice, almost gruff and yet resonating with a deep concern. "Who is it? Who's there?"

The door opened, and I saw the face of a gaunt and bearded old man pressed up against a very thin, full-length cloth – an almost diaphanous door screen which rippled in the breeze. In the darkness, the eerie visage resembled the face of the Turin shroud.

"Who are you?" the veiled figure demanded. "What do you want?"

I stammered out my name and in my nervousness added that I hailed from San Francisco.

"But I don't know anyone, as of late, from San Francisco," the old man replied. "Are you a reporter? If you are, I think you'd better go."

"No, no!" I protested. "I know this sounds strange, but somebody down at the dock said that I should come up and talk to you. He said that you're into philosophy and the arts, things like that."

"I don't know what's going on," said the mysterious greybeard, this time in a softer voice. "But you do seem to look a little tired and hungry. You might as well come on in and have something to eat. And by the way, the name's *Lax*, not Pax. Bob Lax."

The old door of the house creaked fully open, and I entered a dim, short corridor. To my left was a small kitchen which we passed en route to what appeared to be the illuminated main room. Just ahead, a partially closed glass and wood panelled door prevented me from seeing anything clearly until Lax slowly swung it open, and we entered the warm, intensely quiet living space.

For the first time we were in a place of light. I looked at Lax propping open a shutter with an old black shoe and saw him to be unlike any elderly man I had known. His movements were simple, pure, unaffected. His rustic, honest strength was tempered by a gentleness I knew only in nature – the identical peace one might feel in watching a tree sway in the wind. Though agile and alert – far keener than people half his age – he moved about unconscious of his own enlightened being, as if a higher consciousness propelled him. He was unattached to his own authenticity. He was a portal to a higher reality.

I sat down on a couch by the door to take it all in – his being, the room, the concentrated and unfolding energy of the place. Somehow I smelled newly tilled fields and ocean surf. I thrust my hands into warm, dark earth. I could taste wine, and rough, course bread. I could even feel the cotton sweater and worn blue jeans on his lean frame. All at once I knew what it was like to be a seed touched by light or a jagged piece of driftwood cast up onto a sandy beach, nestled in seaweed, bathed in salt and sunshine.

I rested my hands on the couch and took in the entire room. Heavy wooden beams stained with age and candlesoot braced the roof of the late nineteenth-century home. A large round Japanese lantern hung from the ceiling. On the surrounding white walls were postcards, artwork. Behind me, carefully spread out, was a large black-and-white mural of oriental design. Scattered about were a few wooden chairs and tables loaded with books, papers, and many cardboard boxes. A few worn rugs covered the hardwood floor. His small brown bed, flush against the wall, looked austere, spartan. On the far side of the room a light blue door was ajar and through it I glimpsed a small, book-lined study.

The simple home looked well lived-in. It felt like a pair of old leather shoes or a comfortable, time-worn jacket. Good and centred living had gone on here. It seemed the very air was charged with the harmonious life of the dweller. Rich tones permeated everywhere, much like those experienced at sunset. The activity within had left an afterglow.

While the whole place appeared ordinary, almost insignificant from the outside, inside the atmosphere took on an increasingly otherworldly, supernatural quality. I felt as if I had entered a psychic "hot spot," a sacred site somehow meant to help keep the universe in balance. And this feeling intensified with every moment.

As I scanned the rarefied dwelling, I glanced at a few of the postcards on the nearby table. Japan, Austria, Germany, France – they came from the world over. Suddenly I noticed how the numerous boxes in the room were completely filled with correspondence. There were piles of letters everywhere. Standing motionless, Lax had been carefully watching me. "Lots of mail," he said. "I sit around doing nothing and people write me letters, beautiful letters."[12]

Obviously I had chanced upon an extraordinary man. I remember how for a few moments Lax disappeared into his kitchen, and then returned, handing me a yogurt and spoon. A faint smile played upon his lips.

"What brings you to Patmos, Steve?" he quietly asked.

Lax had taken a seat directly opposite me. A narrow wooden table loaded with books, papers, and a few golden origami birds separated us. He had positioned himself near an antique desk lamp, and his deep-set eyes, sometimes sea blue, sometimes grey, then green, were set off by its amber glow.

In that soft, mellow light, the visage of the mysterious sage appeared peaceful, luminous. His lean, ascetic face took on the tranquil radiance of candleflame. His warm, encouraging expression seemed to intone, "Everything is all right. I'm here for you. All that matters is what's happening right now."

Somewhat nervously, and then in a gradually relaxed, easygoing manner, I told him about my recent hardships, to which he intermittently nodded and smiled, almost as if he had heard it all before. He hardly ever blinked, although every so often he lowered his eyes and took long, deep breaths, calmly whispering, "Yes, yes."

When I had finished speaking, Lax bent down his head and said nothing for about a minute. I felt that the quiet might shatter the room. Then his searching, ancient eyes met mine and he said, "Well, son, all I can say is that you've certainly come to the right place to recharge your batteries, that's for sure. Patmos is an isle of love."

As I looked into the old poet's kind and happy eyes, eyes which seemed to laugh and were almost as wide as an owl's, I felt a sudden urge to giggle, and did so. When Lax saw me laugh, he joined in, only he laughed all the harder. So for a time we laughed uninhibitedly like two drunken men. Eventually, though, when things became quiet, he slowly reached behind him and brought forth an old, patched-up notebook wrapped in twine. After delicately opening it, taking care not to tear the yellowed, time-worn pages, he carefully wrote down my name and address, his long, thin articulated fingers wielding the pen like a magician or a meticulous scribe dedicated to every letter.

Then Lax began to ask me about my occupation and interests. After learning that I was a teacher, a writer, and had a fondness for things spiritual, he brought up Thomas Merton and familiarized me with Merton's life and work, yet without revealing the details of his association with the famous monk, except to say that he was his friend. Only after I returned to San Francisco and read *The Seven Storey Mountain* did I come to know the depth of their companionship and Lax's pivotal role in Merton's life.

Following that memorable night, I fast became a devotee of "the poet," and, along with a handful of other young "disciples," periodically walked with him along the wharf of Skala, happy to be in his refreshing, tranquil presence. Lax's rolling, meditative gait, surely cultivated after many years of peripatetic reflection, instilled in me a sense of calm and reverie. Day after day I would go out to him, and follow him, and in the golden Aegean light would receive spirit-lessons by the sea.

During this time I began to observe how Lax was endowed with what might be termed "highly developed extrasensory abilities." At times, he seemed to hear things that were well out of normal range. And when I would approach him with a question, he seemed to anticipate my thoughts and quickly ask, "What was that?" There were also moments when he sensed that a certain person would be coming along to see him or was within the immediate area. He also saw things almost too difficult to see; one day when we were walking together, he bent down to remove a tiny, half-buried needle from the road, afraid that it might injure a child. Moreover, while his movements were usually meditative and slow, he all at once could move very quickly if required to do so. And perhaps the strangest thing about this mystic was that he might say a few words that had no apparent meaning, yet days later, their wisdom could be applied to a particular situation, indicating his possible clairvoyance. Of course Lax, in his perpetual modesty, would vehemently deny these claims or would whimsically ascribe them to "good listening" and "healthy living."

Following my 1993 visit to Patmos, I regularly returned to the isle in order to continue what Lax and I had come to call our "student–teacher relationship." Each time I went back to see "Uncle Robo," as he was affectionately addressed by his friends, I felt recharged, born again by his presence and words. Indeed, it felt so comforting to know that Lax lived in the world, a graced poet through whom I continued to receive artistic inspiration and the impetus to do good things. Routinely I would journey to the Isle of the Revelation and walk up the old familiar way to his hermitage knowing that he would be there, most likely reading, writing or meditating on his bed, or perhaps gazing out over the sea.

"So you're back again," he would say in his warm, gentle way, his happy eyes bright and smiling. "But Captain

Robo," I'd reply ("Captain" owing to his love of the sea), "you know I have to keep coming back. You make the best soul food in the Mediterranean!" And we'd laugh aloud for a while, much like on the first night that I met him. Then, after he gave a sign that it would be good to sit down, we'd take our respective seats at the narrow wooden table in his main room.

Always smiling, sometimes faintly humming, he would slowly pour me a glass of bottled water into one of two mugs that were usually on the table, and then fill his own cup with equal care. Perhaps nothing would be said at first, but eventually a sound, a poem, an artwork or an impression would spark an exchange, and there would be a rich flow of meditative, constructive thought. Periodic silences would follow, to which we both listened almost as if the quiet were a third party speaking to us. And in response to that stillness we would breathe deeply, come to a sort of relaxed attention, and in a humble, reverent manner lower our eyes, as though acknowledging the mystical presence of something greater.

Over the years, I came to see how Lax, more than any other individual, had best instructed me on how to live. He always had a gift for awakening the spiritual and creative potential in people and pointing them in the right direction. His sensitivity and spontaneity demonstrated that he flowed with a loving and overarching wisdom.

Since his days at Columbia University, he proved himself to be a man worth listening to.

Lax entered my life when I needed to establish a holistic foundation on which to grow – a definitive, imperishable centre from which to expand and continue the second half of my existence. My college students had repeatedly asked me how to most skillfully live, and I wanted my answers to be based on experience. Already in my thirties, I was at a point of transition and sought a role model who could teach me how to age well, and not grow "old." I needed a guide, a sage to help me in my soul searching or at least give me the confidence that a harmonic sense of balance in this life could be personally attained and shared with others. Though a practising Christian, I desired a more direct means of enlightenment. I wanted to show myself to a master as I was, in all my strengths and weaknesses, in order that I might become stronger. If it were possible to gain illumination through simply reading sacred writings, then more saints would exist, and the earth would approximate paradise. But the spiritual transformation process seemed to indicate that serious aspirants needed to learn first-hand from enlightened wisdom teachers, spiritual guides, *Dreamcatchers*, who, through their virtuous presence and example, would help their disciples to discover unique paths of freedom.[13] Surely this inspirational guidance remains necessary, for the way of the heart which leads to both self-discovery and to a greater understanding of God periodically tests one's inner fortitude. Therefore, in those "dark nights of the soul," where even words and commands may dissolve, the disciple remembers his teacher – someone who with wisdom and compassion had once reached out to help him – and immediately he takes his hand again and is drawn into the light.

On meeting Robert Lax, I knew that I had found a lightgiver. Being in this graced poet's company over an extended period of time has helped me to discover my place in a world that oftentimes seems hollow and corrupt. And though Robert has crossed over to the other shore, he continues to instruct me, not only through his writing but especially in the way that I remember him walking, talking, and attending to the affairs of the day. Truly, the life and art of this "holy acrobat" have spread the joy of life's "spiritual circus" throughout the world. *The Way of the Dreamcatcher* is meant to help in this dissemination.

After
his
act

the
juggler

crossed
the
road

quietly
lightly
in
a
slim
white
suit:

a
moving
pillar

a
path
of
light
in
the
darkness.[14]

S.T. Georgiou
San Francisco
January 2001

[1] Thomas Merton. *The Seven Storey Mountain*. New York: Harcourt Brace, 1948, 181, 237. For a concise introduction to Merton, see *Living with Wisdom: A Life of Thomas Merton* by Jim Forest, New York: Orbis, 1992.

[2] *New York Times Review of Books*, Feb. 5, 1978, and printed in *The ABC's of Robert Lax*, 183. David Miller and Nicholas Zurbrugg, Editors. Exeter: Stride, 1999. This is the most thorough book in existence on Lax, containing essays on Lax's biography and writing. Also of note is Stride's *Robert Lax: Speaking into Silence* (Garlitz-Loydell-Zurbrugg), 2001.

[3] *The ABC's of Robert Lax*, 66.

[4] Thomas Merton. *The Seven Storey Mountain*, 180–181.

[5] Thomas Merton. *The Seven Storey Mountain*, 237–238. Lax also believed that the way one seeks to become a more "saintly" person, aside from simply "desiring it," is through the proper and necessary stimulus. According to Merton, Lax thought America to be "A country full of people who want to be kind, pleasant, happy, who want to do good and loving things and serve God, but do not know how. And they do not know where to turn to find out. They are surrounded by all kinds of sources of information which only conspire to bewilder them… Lax's vision is a vision of the day when they will turn on the radio and somebody will start telling them what they have really been wanting to hear and what they need to know." (*The Seven Storey Mountain*, New York: Harcourt Brace, 1948, 237).

[6] *The ABC's of Robert Lax*, 190.

[7] Catherine Doherty. *Not Without Parables: Stories of Yesterday, Today, and Eternity*. Notre Dame: Ave Maria Press, 1977, 76–79. Catherine de Hueck Doherty, originally an aristocrat, was a refugee of the Russian Revolution. She began working with the poor and disadvantaged during the Great Depression and opened Catholic Friendship Houses in Harlem, Chicago and Toronto. Eventually, she established the Madonna House Lay Apostolate in 1947, based in Combermere, Ontario, which functions to this day.

Robert Lax and Steve Georgiou shortly after their first meeting in the summer of 1993.

Skala, the port town of Patmos. Arrival by night is particularly moving. As the ferry slowly circles the island, one sees the lights of Hora, the mountaintop village that clusters around the medieval monastery of St. John, twinkle like stars in the darkness. Minutes later, the boat turns past a great promontory and the sweeping radiance of Skala welcomes the traveller in an almost magical way.

Looking out from a monk's cell in the Monastery of St. John the Theologian. Framed within the small window are the gates of Patmos Bay.

The twelfth-century Monastery of St. John the Theologian looming above the village of Hora. Below is the Monastery of the Apocalypse, in the recesses of which lies the sacred cave and grotto where, according to Eastern Orthodox tradition, St. John witnessed the Revelation. Numerous theologians of the early Church saw John the Disciple, Evangelist, Theologian and Seer as one and the same.

"Go up, and you will find his house." En route to Robert Lax's hermitage, situated near Mt. Kastelli.

The narrow, winding streets of Patmos. "The clean whitewashed homes stood out of the darkness and guided me onward and upward…"

Robert Lax's hermitage.

Lax opening gifts in the hermitage. "Most of what I have
– almost everything – has been given or sent to me by
friends."

⁸ See in this book the first dialogue section, "Origins." Kerouac also referred to Lax as a "good saint" (*The Beat Vision*, A. Knight, ed., New York, Paragon, 1987, 112). And in a revealing letter to the Beat poet Philip Whalen dated February 2, 1961, Kerouac wrote, "Robert Lax, a Jewish guy who is a Catholic convert of a sort, in any case a strange wonderful laughing Buddha. Laughs all the time. Is Editor of the Catholic magazine *Jubilee*, and the best friend of Thomas Merton the Trappist Divine" (*Jack Kerouac: The Selected Letters: 1957–1969*, ed. by Ann Charters, Penguin Books, 1999, 321). Interestingly, Kerouac signed a letter to Joyce Johnson, dated January 1958, as Jack "Lax" (*Door Wide Open: Jack Kerouac and Joyce Johnson: A Beat Love Affair in Letters 1957–1958.* New York: Penguin Books, 2000, 116).

⁹ Robert Lax. *Journal B.* Switzerland: Pendo-Verlag, 1988, 72. Prior to 1985, many of Lax's writings were published by small presses such as Journeyman Books and appeared in booklet form through Michael Lastnight's Furthermore Press. However, Pendo Verlag of Switzerland, under the direction of Bernard Moosbrugger, has faithfully published Lax's poetry and journals for the past twenty years in English-German bilingual editions. In the past decade, more Lax titles have been published in America such as *33 Poems.* New York: New Directions, 1988; *Love Had A Compass: The Journals and Poetry of Robert Lax.* Edited by James Uebbing. New York: Grove Press, 1996; *A Thing That Is: New Poems.* Edited by Paul Spaeth, New York: Overlook Press, 1997; *Circus Days and Nights.* Edited by Paul Spaeth. New York: Overlook Press, 2001. Lax has been featured in a recent book by Peter France titled *Hermits: The Insights of Solitude.* New York: St. Martin's Press, 1996. Brother Patrick Hart, O.C.S.O., last secretary to Thomas Merton, has written *Patmos Journal: In Search of Thomas Merton With Robert Lax,* Ring Tarigh, 1996. The complete letters of Lax and Merton have recently been published by the University Press of Kentucky: *When Prophecy Still Had A Voice.* Edited by Arthur W. Biddle, 2001. Additionally, the Spring 2001 issue of *The Merton Seasonal* is entirely devoted to Lax and includes a wide array of essays and articles on Lax written by his close friends and admirers.

[10] Martin Buber. *The Origin and Meaning of Hasidism.* Edited and translated by Maurice Friedman. New York: Horizon, 1960, 181.

[11] Examples of Lax's "off the wall" humour may be found in *A Catch of Anti-Letters.* Kansas City, MO: Sheed and Ward, 1978. Merton edited this fascinating collection of correspondence between Lax and himself prior to his accidental death in Thailand in 1968. With regard to Lax functioning as an unassuming "channel of higher energy," a comparison with Chuang Tzu's "Man of Te" is apt:

> When the enlightened king rules
> His deeds spread over the whole world
> but seem not from himself;
> His riches are loaned to the myriad things
> but the people do not depend on him.
> He is there, but no one mentions his name.
> He lets things find their own delight.

Chuang Tzu. *The Inner Chapters.* Translated by A.C. Graham. London: Mandala, 1986, 96.

[12] The holy atmosphere of Lax's home relates with a minor incident that took place in his hermitage some years after I had met him. On the night that I was to leave Patmos in 1997, he pointed to a pack of postcards and suggested that I take one as a memory of my most recent visit. The yellow and blue card I had selected displayed large-sized Chinese calligraphy. Upon returning, I looked up the characters, which together read "Jade Roof." In Chinese symbolism, "jade" represents strength, honesty, harmony and virtue. When combined with the character "roof," a hut is typically inferred, and not just an ordinary hut, but one that is most prized and sacred. Indeed, when placing the character "jade" beneath "roof," the word "precious" is formed. In essence, the card seemed to point to a very special and sacred dwelling: Lax's hermitage, truly a "Jade Roof."

[13] A common belief among old world cultures has it that the quality of what the disciple understands largely depends upon the quality of the sage speaking. In essence, illumination proceeds not only from the

teacher's words, but exudes from the purity and harmony of his very being. Therefore the mere presence of the teacher helps to spontaneously generate enlightenment. See "Master and Disciple: Two Religio-Sociological Studies" by Joachim Wach, in *The Journal of Religion*, Volume XLII, No. 1, January 1962.

[14] Robert Lax. *Mogador's Book*. Switzerland: Pendo-Verlag, 1969. 74.

ORIGINS

And in the beginning was love.
Love made a sphere.
All things grew within it.
The sphere then encompassed
beginnings and endings,
beginning and end.
Love had a compass
whose whirling dance traced out
a sphere of love in the void;
in the center thereof
rose a fountain.

Robert Lax,
from *Circus of the Sun*

Robert Lax was born in 1915 in Olean, a town in western New York. He entered Columbia University in 1932, where he majored in English literature. At Columbia, he became part of a remarkable circle of prolific, imaginative friends whose free-wheeling creativity and diverse interests may have helped to initiate the subsequent "Beat Generation." Among this eclectic group of writers and artists were Thomas Merton, Ad Reinhardt, Edward Rice, and John Berryman. Early admirers of Lax included Jack Kerouac, Allen Ginsberg, Lawrence Ferlinghetti, e.e. cummings, and Denise Levertov.

After graduating from Columbia, Lax continued his writing, briefly remaining in Manhattan, where he made friends with many artists and musicians. Then he began a long period of wandering, moving to North Carolina, Connecticut, California and Canada. Along the way, various types of employment were to follow. He worked as a bartender, a night watchman, coached juvenile boxers, did ad-copy work at a radio station, and taught English classes at the University of North Carolina. This academic appointment did not last long, however, because he gave his students A's simply for making the effort to attend class.

Lax also became an editor at *The New Yorker*, followed a circus, founded the peace publication *PAX*, wrote film reviews for *Time*, and signed on as a scriptwriter at the Samuel Goldwyn Studio in Hollywood. Some years after his brief career in the motion picture industry, Lax was appointed "roving editor" of the liberal Catholic magazine *Jubilee*, which took him to various parts of Europe. After spending time in France, he visited Greece in 1962, and in 1964 returned there to stay. At first he remained on the Aegean island of Kalymnos and then moved to nearby Patmos, a quiet, ascetic isle situated just off the Turkish coastline where he lived an eremitical existence for many decades.

By 1959, Lax had published his first collection of lyrical poetry, *Circus of the Sun*, illustrated by his friend Emil Antonucci, the graphic artist who had founded Hand Press and Journeyman Books, through which Lax published much of his early work. However, shortly before moving to the Greek isles, Lax turned to a simple, minimalist writing style meant to focus attention on the pure contemplation of words and images as seen in *New Poems* (1962) and *Sea and Sky* (1965). Although minimalist writing and art had been anticipated in the neo-expressionist movements of Dada, Futurism, and later in Concrete Poetry, Lax's work remains unique because of its simultaneously abstract and visual quality.

Lax was drawn to write in the minimalist, "less is more" style for many reasons. To begin, interest in reductionism was common to his artistic generation, which included John Cage, William Burroughs, and Abstract Expressionist painters such as Ad Reinhardt. However, Lax had always been inspired by simplicity – how basic elements in both art and life shape meaning. When as a child he first saw Constantin Brancusi's "Bird In Space," he was greatly moved by its simple, abstract beauty. And in 1939, while the young poet and his Columbia friends enjoyed an earthy, creative summer in a wilderness cottage outside of Olean, Lax felt an intense desire to write simply, and of simple things.

This early dedication to simplicity may readily be seen in Lax's rustic manner of living after college. He seemed most himself among the poor and those practising a grass-roots lifestyle. Lax worked with the disadvantaged in Harlem, lived in the slums of Marseille, and befriended gypsies in Europe. And when Lax moved to the barren Greek isles of Kalymnos and Patmos, he intensified a lifelong practice of Zen and Yoga, which both stress economy and purity of form. Finally, in studying Haiku and Eastern philosophy, as well as Jewish mystical works such as the Kabbalah, Lax was impressed with how much could be said with a few choice words.

A Star to Steer By

Captain Robo! It's so good to see you again. I've visited you so many times, and I just keep coming back.

Good seeing you again too, old boy! And I hope you keep coming back – come here every time you can! How was the boat ride from Piraeus?

Great weather, considering winter is just around the corner. Hazy blue skies, calm seas. And on the way over, I was reflecting about the things I want to ask you, having to do with your life, work, and spiritual beliefs.

All of that sounds good to me. Those categories are certainly interrelated… Let's get the cameras rolling!

OK. All quiet on the set! Lights, camera, action! (Laughter). – So I'd like to start by asking you about your ethnic origins.

That's a good beginning. Well, my roots are Austrian and Polish. Some of my parents' relatives had their roots in Vienna and some in Krakow. And I think it's been recently discovered that our family was of Sephardic Jewish ancestry, so the roots go back to Spain, most likely. There are Laxes in Spain and Laxes even in Turkey, and they are of Sephardic origin.

You were born into a Jewish family and practised Judaism faithfully. Then, in your mid-twenties, you converted to Christianity, to Catholicism. What was the catalyst?

My feeling was that after carefully reading Isaiah and the Prophets of the Old Testament, the coming of the Redeemer, the Messiah was indeed prophesied. He would have all kinds of good qualities which Jesus seemed to embody. He would be the Prince of Peace, the Sustainer of Love, and so on. Yet when He came, some people rejected Him. I certainly didn't want to be counted as one opposing Him – I just didn't want to identify with those who had turned Him away. I simply wanted to participate with Him as a peacemaker.

What did your parents think of your conversion?

They were wonderful, my goodness, just so wonderful and supportive. However, my mother, Betty, first asked me to think it over for a year and live the Jewish faith as best I could. A year went by, and my desire to convert was still strong, so I received her blessing. And my older sister Gladys – who knew that my spiritual interests were serious and had been for quite a while – simply shrugged her shoulders in a divine way and said, "Well, I think you can pray just as well on your knees as with your hat on." My father Sigmund wrote me a beautiful letter about my conversion, and congratulated me on having found what I wanted to do. I remember one thing he said in the letter, though, and that was not to convert any Jewish boys.

What Jewish elements do you cherish in Christianity?

I guess all of them that are there...

As you were growing up, did you ever feel that you had a destiny?

(Laughter). I've had good dreams. Most of us do, in one form or another.

Speaking of dreams, I've noticed a new addition to your home. There's a dreamcatcher up there hanging just above your bed. That malachite stone in the centre really catches the light.

Yes, that was given to me by a friend. It's a North American Indian creation meant to filter out the bad dreams and keep in the good ones, at least according to Lakota tradition. And it seems to be doing its job. I like it up there – its gentle feather just seems to float.

What do dreams mean to you?

I've certainly had a lifelong interest in them. Like they say in Tibetan Buddhism, dreams prepare us for the day. In a way, they condition us. Providing we get enough sleep, they do their best to tell us more about the real persons that we are. Dreams take us out of the ping-pong games of the day. In them we enter an awakening stream.[1]

So we learn from all-knowing night?

Yes, that's good. As Jung tells us, the states of sleeping and waking are deeply and mysteriously interconnected.[2] They exchange charges just like we do. I think dreams can be lighthouses in the communal sea of consciousness. Perhaps we are more awake when we're asleep. (Laughter). Dreams seem so much like pathways of light, like stars to steer by.

Is humanity one great dreaming organism?

It's true. While we're all involved in our own special dreams, together we are part of one big flowing dream that ends and begins in heaven.

How can we learn more about that big dream?

By being creative, I think, since heaven, like earth, is a creative place. I believe all artists help us to understand the dream, as well as everyone who is a lover, a giver of love and life.

Do you trust your dreams?

I listen to all of them, as many as I can remember. If they suggest that I do good things, I try to do the good suggested. But if I'm not sure, I think I might be inclined to talk about it with someone whom I trust. The Spanish mystic St. John of the Cross[3] said for us to weigh our dreams carefully. A lot of wise people have said the same thing.

You know, every time I see you, you always seem to be wearing something blue, and you oftentimes wear rough-cut work clothes, as if you were a fisherman. Why?

I like to wear the colour blue, both dark and light. And I'd better wear rough clothes because I'm always getting them creased and torn. Of course, I have more decent clothes should I need them. Over the years here I've gone to weddings and things like that.

I remember you telling me how the fishermen of Patmos tend to wear blue, whereas the farmers typically wear brown.

That's fairly true.

Does your preference for blue point to your love of nature? Are you more of a "fisherman" than a farmer?

I've always loved the sea. Many fishing folk are my friends. Sure, you can say that.

Blue is a healing colour.

Most certainly. Many amulets here in the Mediterranean are blue-toned. It's a tranquil colour.

And the therapeutic qualities of blue are known throughout the world. In fact, the Madonna's symbolic colour is blue.

Oh yes, you're so right there.

And there's a window decoration of a blue lion right nearby your home which always reminds me of your many cats. Tell me, what do cats mean to you?

Cats?

You have twenty, don't you? And you've named them all! I saw them outside as I was coming in.

Actually, I only have eighteen now. But they do have what seems to me to be a very good intuitive sense. They communicate clearly and perceptively with their eyes. They tend to get along with each other, whether or not they have a reason to. When you think they're asleep, they're actually awake. They're light on their feet. They can remain motionless for such a long time. Although they're seldom known as "man's best friend," I think they are. I guess I'm a cat person.

Speaking of cats, is your personality more "cataphatic" (God is knowable, as through love) or "apophatic" (God is ultimately unknowable)?

Meow. (Laughter). Actually, I believe it's both. It's natural to have both of those things happening from moment to moment as we go through life.

When you went to Columbia University for your Bachelor of Arts degree, you, Merton, Ad Reinhardt, Ed Rice, Bob Gibney, Bob Gerdy, John Slate, and Sy Freedgood were part of an arts and literary circle that worked on the school publication, The Jester. *What was that like?*

Truly the best bunch of guys. We had an absolutely great time. It was one of those pinnacle experiences. Lots of genuine joy and love. Maybe some headaches too. (Laughter). Really brings on the music. And we pretty much kept in touch after college.

What were your first impressions of Merton?

Positively electric. We met at the John Jay Dining Hall at Columbia. Herb Jacobson, the editor of *The Jester*, took me over to meet him. He looked up. Like I've said so many times before, it was one of the best glances upward. I'll never forget that smile, his handshake…pure joy.

You encouraged Merton to "become a saint." Did you apply the same philosophy to yourself?

Well, I've always tried to be a good boy. But I think that whole thing came about through a question I put to Merton which was, "What do you want to be – a good Catholic or a saint?" I suggested to him that what everyone should be, given a choice, is a saint, a holy person. By saint, we don't mean a canonized saint, or a saint of any particular denomination; we simply mean a holy person. We are meant to be holy, all of us are. We're all called to be saints. Now someone once wrote, "The worst thing Lax could have done was to tell Merton to be a saint." But Merton knew what I meant, and, what's more, he went out and just about became the saint he was called to be. I mean, he's mighty close.

It's known that both you and Merton had a good deal of Franciscan influence. Did it start at St. Bonaventure University in New York?

With regard to Merton, I took him out to the school, and he found the place quite appealing. As for myself, I grew up right near the campus, and the Franciscans seemed like pretty peaceful people. And my mother had taken courses there when I was growing up, so I knew about the school from a young age. Later in life I visited the university for various reasons, and so got to know the campus better. I also used the library there, Friedsam Library, and read many books on St. Francis of Assisi, of whom I was especially fond, and still am. It was there that

I met the wonderful friar Ireneaus Herscher, whom I later introduced to Merton...[4] But I should add that at the same time that I was engaged in Franciscan studies, I had a good deal of interest in St. Thomas Aquinas and later began a dissertation on him at the University of North Carolina which I never completed, owing to other interests.[5]

Who was the closest person to you before college?

Certainly my dear mother Betty, who instilled in me a love of the arts. Also my older sister Gladio (Gladys). Yes, I think that's right.

A few years after graduating from Columbia, you, Merton, Rice, Slate, Gibney, and others in your arts circle at Columbia went off to a cottage in Olean and engaged in what may be termed a bohemian lifestyle, where writing, playing music, and the study of philosophy was the norm. Writers have termed this period as "Proto Beat" and even "Proto-Hippie." Do you think that you and your college friends helped to initiate the Beat Movement?

Whether or not we were the precursors of the Beats, I don't know. Maybe one generation just led smoothly into the next. Maybe that sort of thing was going on in various parts of the country. A lot of people were on the same wavelength. But certainly we were the only ones who showed up at the country club with blue jeans and beards! (Laughter). We were held together by the kind of stuff that we enjoyed – writing, meditation, drumming, singing, jazz – all of those expressive things. So we were simply continuing what we had done at Columbia. Of course, by this time we already had a taste of the commercial world, and we didn't go for it. To get ahead meant that you had to conform to standards that seemed hollow.

Speaking of the Beats, you've told me that you and Jack Kerouac were good friends. In a way, you were his mentor. He wrote about you being "a pilgrim in search of beautiful innocence."[6]

Oh yes, Kerouac and I got along just fine – we hit it off just right, we were good friends. We exchanged letters, went to bookstores, cafés, even went cat shopping one day. I liked his writing and I liked him. Lots of energy. We used to talk into the wee hours of the morning on all sorts of things, mainly religion. He called me, "Laughing Buddha," and I addressed him as "Jackie Kerouackie." Later, Kerouac introduced me to Allen Ginsberg, his Columbia classmate. They both knew about our arts circle at Columbia, and they had gone on to create their own. When I met Ginsberg, the first thing he said was, "Do you believe in God?" I replied, "I'm a Catholic." Three years later, Ginsberg telephoned me to see how I was doing, and the first thing he said was, "Are you still a Catholic?" I thought that was pretty funny.

Did any of the group in retreat at Olean ever engage in psychedelic substances, as would happen in the Beat generation? Were drugs used to explore or enhance creativity?

Well, marijuana was certainly out there, and a lot of people had begun to experiment with it. But as far as our own group, none of us were really into pot. It just wasn't necessary. We were more into what we enjoyed doing, and anything that took us too far away from the pure joy of creation and contemplation we just didn't do. Sure, we drank every now and then, but not to excess. I mean, we didn't get completely smashed every night. We'd drive over to Bradford for an evening of drinking and come back in the early morning, and I never had the slightest worry about any of us not making it back home. Ed Rice usually drove, since Merton and I didn't drive – not even in a backseat fashion – and Rice was a good navigator.[7]

Like Merton, Ed Rice was very close to you, and I believe that he was instrumental in your baptism.

Yes, he was my godfather, and he was Merton's godfather too. He was a brilliant man who started *Jubilee* magazine in 1953, which some say was the most creative Catholic publication ever published in America. Rice understood my wanderlust, and eventually appointed me "Roving Editor," which allowed me to travel at will. Prior to this I had been working at *Time, Parade,* and *The New Yorker.*

Circus Roberto

I know that while you were working at The New Yorker, *you suddenly decided to follow a travelling circus through western Canada – The Cristiani Brothers. You wrote a long poem about the experience titled* Circus of the Sun, *where the circus becomes a metaphor for creation. What made you leave everything and follow a circus?*

Well, one day, the Cristiani Family Circus came to town. I went to interview them for *The New Yorker.* They were the most remarkable people I had ever run into. They invited me to go with them on their tour, so I saddled up and joined them. I was truly blessed to have met the family.

I know that you learned about juggling through the circus, something you have always liked to do. What does juggling do for you?

Perhaps more than any other circus art, it does depend on being focused on the present moment. You really have to know what you are doing in the immediate here and now. There is no lingering in the past or future – there is only the present. It is the art of the now.

This sounds like Zen.

Metaphorically speaking, yes.

Did you ever participate in the circus acts?

Yes, I was a clown at times. It was a lot of fun.

You still love clowns —

And clownin' around.

(Laughter). Right! But does your devotion to clowns have anything to do with humility? It's not unusual for clowns to appear foolish so as to elicit laughter in their audience.

Being a clown may relate to that idea. It takes love, joy, talent, energy, and, yes, even a bit of humility to be a clown. I really do feel that clowns must have the spiritual insight to be clowns.

Like Christ, clowns bring joy.

They bring joy, but there are different kinds of clowns — the ones that act aggressive and ask different types of questions, the ones that don't know anything, the ones that are sad, the ones that are exuberant…

Recently I learned that Circus Days and Nights, *another book on your time spent with a travelling circus, is about to come out.*

Yes, this has to do with a circus I followed in Italy. It will also include my poem "Voyage to Pascara."

Tell me, can Patmos be likened to a circus?

How so, Steve?

On this sacred isle God is the Ringmaster, as demonstrated by the medieval Monastery of St. John which dominates this place.[8] Each day the ferry boat brings in new performers who enter the centre ring.

And don't you have a sign in your entryway reading "Circus Roberto"?

That's very good. I can see that. Yes, Patmos may be likened to the circus in this way because it transmits the universal language of joy.

Some years before your circus experience, you were involved with Hollywood. You went to Los Angeles and became a scriptwriter at the Samuel Goldwyn studios. How did that start, and did you write any scripts that were made into movies?

I had been invited by the director Arthur Ripley to come to Hollywood. Eventually I did, and yes, one script which I wrote with Rowland Leigh titled *The Siren of Atlantis* was made into a film. It was based on a novel by Pierre Benoit.

Didn't you act in a movie yourself?

That's true. But that happened later, and it was not in Los Angeles, but Greece. I had a very minor role, nothing came of it, and the film was never released. Merton playfully chided me about that for a while.[9]

Why did you leave Hollywood after a few years? Was the climate corrupting your soul?

Let me think. As time passed, I saw that Hollywood was the wrong place for me. Yes, there was a lot to like; it was an imaginative arena, and I'm sure it was all part of the plan that I should be there. But by the time I got back to New York, man, I was ready to kiss the sidewalk. Yet, as I said, there were some good things in Hollywood too. For instance, my uncle, Harry Hotchner, a banker and the real estate manager of Charlie Chaplin, lived in the area. He had many spiritual interests and was a staunch Theosophist, one of the people who had adopted and brought up Krishnamurti. But at the same, he kept his feet on the ground.[10]

Did your uncle hold a high position in the Theosophical Society of America?

Both my uncle and aunt had prominent roles, but they weren't at the level of Madam Blavatsky.[11] My uncle's picture was up on the wall at our home in New York, and of my mother's two brothers, I could sense that he was the favoured one, the most admired of the two. I used to like looking at the photograph as I was growing up, knowing that one day I'd meet him. And another good thing – he always sent us fruitcake during Christmas time.

So your uncle was a mentor to you?

Yes, he was. He was a great support. Every night, after I returned home from the studio, he would phone me and talk over spiritual problems and important questions which I had been thinking about at that time. Should I leave Hollywood, go to Harlem, and work for the poor? Should I teach at a university? That sort of thing.

Have you had other mentors?

Many people I've met, corresponded with over the years have had an influence on me. Teachers at Columbia like Mark Van Doren,[12] Jacques Barzun.[13] And certainly Merton, Ad Reinhardt,[14] Dorothy Day,[15] Jacques Maritain,[16] Jean Vanier,[17] Brahmachari…I really do think Brahmachari was a mentor, and still is. He continues to write beautiful letters to me. I remember his bright yellow turban and blue sneakers. We used to take long walks together and eat vegetarian food. He truly was an emissary of peace, a beautiful soul. Through him I learned so much about India and about the joy of being alive in love.[18]

This is Brahmachari, the colourful Hindu holy man mentioned in Merton's The Seven Storey Mountain *who came to New York on a spiritual mission. He needed a place to stay, and after meeting him, you secretly brought him into your dormitory at Columbia where he lived for a while. How old is he now?*

He must be 93 or 94, at least. He lives in his ashram near Calcutta. And what he did when he turned 93 was to go out into the market and distribute blankets to the poor.

Great move. What a way to celebrate a birthday — to give on the very day you were given life, sort of like returning the favour.

Yes, and what I suddenly remember about him is how he spoke of his own mentor's passing. His teacher – Jagad-Bondhu, which I think means "World-Binder," had died, and as he was lying in his coffin, the mourners gathered about him and said how even in death Jagad was not idle – his remains were sustaining biological life, feeding insects and other critters.

Brahmachari sounds like a fascinating man.

Yes, he was a wonderful dancer too! He would lead people out to where the lowest caste members – the "Untouchables" – lived in town and he would dance with them. Often he would make an Untouchable the lead dancer in the group. He loved to spread happiness. He really believed that we praise God according to how we live.

Did Brahmachari expose you to Hindu spirituality?

Certainly Brahmachari had endeared Merton and myself to the ways of India, but what Merton and I both noted about Brahmachari was that he encouraged us to find enlightenment within our own Western religious traditions, which he thought were excellent spiritual systems. I remember one book he liked a lot was St. Augustine's *Confessions*. You see, he was not a proselytizer, seeking to convert the West – he just wanted to awaken people to a higher power operating in the universe and help them to flow with it. He felt that since he was already living in the presence of God – as we all do – this was the most anybody could ask for. So he decided to trust God in all things, and he lived his entire life that way.

God will provide.

Yes, exactly.

Go with the Flow

With time, your interests turned more and more toward Greece. Is it true that you were drawn to Greece partly because you liked the Greek restaurants of New York?

That's right. At other restaurants, they would briskly ask, "What do you want?" But at the Greek places they would ask, with all sincerity, "How do you feel?" And I remember a waiter who had a classic Greek profile who stood beneath an olive tree in an outdoor café. It all pointed to a Greek odyssey, particularly when I found myself stopping at luggage shops and staring at the suitcases as if I was mesmerized.

Before Greece you went to Marseille and lived among the poor. Why?

Actually, before Marseille, I went to Paris, like all young artists. It was the thing to do. Not to go to Paris was not to have lived! On my first trip I was about 21, and went with one of my classmates, John Slate. Afterwards we went to Venice too. It was a kind of a "Fred Astaire Grand Tour."

Wasn't it during this trip that you and Slate communicated solely in dog barks?

That was our language for part of the trip, during the train ride. (Laughter). A Japanese passenger who overheard us gave us a compliment and said that we barked well.

This reminds me of a game you and Merton played on the New York subway system. When the train picked up speed, you and he would enter a feigned mystic trance. Your "altered states" would intensify or subside according to the pace of the train.

Sure, we did something like that as we zipped along. (Laughter). But getting back to France, what surprised me was that, more than Paris, Marseille made the greatest impact upon me. At first I thought I didn't like it, but afterwards I decided to go back. I found it to be a place where the exercise of charity went a long way.[19]

What is interesting about your many travels is that you seem to prefer poor, rustic, out of the way locales. Your living in a Catholic settlement for the poor in Harlem, in the down-and-out areas along the Marseille waterfront, on barren Greek isles, and even among gypsies seems to indicate that you are drawn to remote, impoverished places. As well, your minimalist poems are ascetic in style. Do you consciously live in environments which mirror your "less is more" nature?

Well, I do think you're right. Whatever turmoil I was experiencing in my younger days, whatever changes were transpiring in my attempts to live a simpler life, I found it all at Marseille. It's not unusual to consciously or subconsciously enter an environment that appears to be an extension of your own inner being, especially if your intent is to reflect and create. Inevitably, though, we find the place that is right for us, where our natures harmonize with our surroundings. The "catkins" outside know when they have found a good spot to lie back and be comfortable. They don't have to be told where to go.

What if you can't find a place that fosters creativity or is a larger reflection of your balanced being?

I think you should value those moments. They are still a part of your evolution. If you keep finding yourself in bad places, there's a reason why you're there. The time comes to figure out why, and in a calm, fluid way. That's why the best thing you can do in living is to welcome each moment as it comes along, because every moment has meaning. But don't freeze frame the moment – with understanding and appreciation let it pass! If you clutch at anything, the whole rhythm gets broken, and you can't grow. Just be patient, be gentle, especially with yourself. Every moment is a gift and so is the flow through which the moments go, so you let the moments come, you let the moments go. You just gotta let go to ride the flow.

Hey, all of that rhymes!

Well, that's poetry, son. (Laughter). You see, the whole thing amounts to our receptivity of both the good and the bad moments. If you fixate on the good or bad moments, then the big freeze happens – your mind will be taken up by your fixations, and you will lose track of the flow. That's what you never want to do if you can help it, that is, to block the flow. Instead, go with it. Now *"Go with the flow"* may be a cliché, and when I first thought

75

about it, the phrase kind of put me off, but as time passed, I found it to be quite valuable, a very wise way to live. It's sort of like listening to music. You don't hang onto each note – you just let them all go right along. When you watch a movie, every clip goes right on by.

Well, being a Californian who loves the beach, I can relate. Some surfers have told me how since the waves are always flowing, what makes the ride most sweet is what kind of wax you put on your board.

Marvellous! Yes, just let the flow go as best as you can manage, no matter how you feel. Let it go right along, and you're well on your way to doing things right. You'll be able to see the whole sea, and not just focus on the waves that bring you in and out. When you've reached that stage, any notion of "self" really starts to disappear. You are simply receptive, awake, open, riding what's happening now. You're not worried about "wiping out"!

Wow! Kowabunga, Bob! How do you know all that mysterioso surfer lingo? You're way into the curl – you're stoked! (Laughter). But really, Merton said that too often we are self-conscious, not conscious.

That's right. A garden hose isn't conscious of itself. It just keeps on watering the plants whenever the water passes through it. It's good when the self disappears. That's why I think we have an idea of self in the first place, so that when we are not self-preoccupied, we know that we are moving on to a better situation. We're catching the next wave.

Are you talking about getting rid of the personality as well as the ego here?

Not at all. We're all supposed to be "ourselves" – that's why we were created as individuals. We're all unique and infinitely special. We all have gifts to discover and share, and in sharing ride the flow where it takes us. I mean, while we're interrelated and part of a greater whole, each of us simultaneously *is* in our own way. That's why when you get to heaven's gate, the angels aren't going to ask you, "Were you as good as Moses?" They're going to ask, "Were you as good as Steve Georgiou?"

So it's important to understand who you are, otherwise you can't fulfill your potential. You have no reference point.

That's pretty much the case. And one of the best ways to come to "know yourself" is in a place of meditative quiet, sort of like this isle.

Would you then loosely call yourself a "Hesychast," one who, according to Eastern Orthodox tradition, "descends into the heart" and remains in quiet prayer so as to better perceive the Spirit at work in oneself and the cosmos?

Sounds good.

Since you knew that you always had a strong spiritual and contemplative inclination, did you ever wish to enter a monastery, as did Merton?

No, and that's because of the three monastic vows: Poverty, Chastity, and Obedience. *Poverty*, I was familiar with. *Chastity*, I could get used to. But one thing I could never get used to was *Obedience*. I don't like being bossed around! Being obedient to a superior really wasn't a part of me. I remember when I graduated from grade school, my mother wrote in my autograph book, "To thine own self be true." So she brought me up, right from the beginning, to be true to myself, and that's an important lesson to get early in life. This reminds me of a story – am I going on too long here?

Please, go right ahead. The stage is yours.

Well, when I was in my twenties, I met a priest who somehow saw that I wasn't the kind of fellow who would dutifully read the Breviary in its entirety on a regular basis. He told me to read two or three Psalms a day, and by doing that, I would experience far more spiritual benefit. And he was right.

Speaking of spiritual advisors, I've heard that you once met the famous holy father and stigmatic Padre Pio[20] and received guidance from him.

He was my confessor.

What was he like? Did you feel that he was special, a saint? I read somewhere that he could bilocate.

Well, he did not bilocate for me. (Laughter). He certainly had stigmata, though. But you know, maybe he did bilocate in a way. You see, he came to me in a dream the night after I had confessed to him in Rome. Yes, he showed up very clearly in a dream, a beautiful dream...

Please go on.

In Rome I had confessed to him in Latin so that he could better understand me. I remember his face afterward, and during Mass — he seemed to be caught up in another world, like a man from the moon. I mean, he really had the innocence and wonder of someone who had never been on earth before, and he radiated a type of otherworldly clarity. And he did give me absolution.

But what about the dream?

The next night, in my dream, he told me, "Now that confession you made was very good, but I want you to go to the nearest Dominican monastery and make your confession in English." So I did. Now that's not standard bilocation, but his appearance and presence seemed so real, so much more tangible than a dream...but, I'm sorry — I took you away from your questions.

No, that was great — a fascinating interlude.

The Isle of Love

Robert, it's been said that you eventually left Marseille and later went on to Greece and Patmos because of a "sign" you saw in your room. Over your bed there was an icon of St. John the Divine writing his

Revelation. This image prompted you to start thinking of Patmos and the famous cave wherein John experienced his vision.

That's a true story. And up there on my wall, among all the other pictures and postcards, is a copy of that very icon. The original is from an illustrated manuscript of the fifteenth century.

Oh yes, there's St. John writing his Apocalypse.

And the fact that he's *writing* also led me to believe that Patmos would be a good place to write and meditate.

So Patmos was love at first sight?

Definitely. Things were clearer here, much more real, rooted, you might say. No distractions. Excellent climate, at least for most months. A fertile, unfolding quiet. Beautiful, inspiring light. Something about the light – so many tones, hues beaming into the soul. And there was also a classical influence as well. It was a ruggedly Homeric place ringed by a "wine dark sea."

What was it that you found holy here? The site must have certainly impressed you since you had previously gone to such inspiring locales as the Virgin Isles, the Canary Isles, and a number of the islands of Italy and Greece.

Many people who visit say that there is an ominous feel to the place as your boat approaches, but not in a bad way. There's just a certain feeling that something spiritually significant is here, waiting to reveal itself in its own good time. When I first came I strongly felt the power of St. John's cave as well as the great monastery and that whole area up there, but it was really the Cave of the Apocalypse[21] that moved me.

You sound just like the islanders — they're very "cave conscious."

Yes, the cave has been a magnet for all the Patmians since the days of St. John. In fact, St. John's association with the cave has permeated the whole psychology of the people here. It has made them loving, gentle, wise. I've found that they never say a word in any situation that doesn't emanate from a pure trust, a deep spiritual centre of which the cave is a part. So many times I've heard, *"Epomoni"* (Patience), *"Oti theli o Theos"* (Whatever God wants) and *"Doxa si o Theos"* (Glory be to God). Everything seems to be right here for a good rapport with the Creator. The men, women and children have a solid spiritual foundation nurtured by the sanctity of the isle and by their forefathers. On top of that, they are always reminded of the high ideals of their classical and Byzantine ancestors. I mean, Socrates' "Know thyself," which many of the locals echo, is a good start for anyone.

So you feel Patmos is truly a sacred site, a blessed zone? Is there a unique energy here? A cosmic pulsing?

I certainly would not be inclined to doubt it. The sun, moon and stars seem to shine right into you. Yes, I very much believe the people are blessed simply by being here.

Grace seems to flow here. You can't help but sense the love of God. The gates of Patmos are as wide as the heart, open to all.

What else did you feel when you first came to this holy isle?

A timeless serenity. Generative silence. Awe. The quiet imposed by the volcanic mountains and stones, a real love moving over the face of the waters. In a more familial sense, I did feel like someone might if they had run into their long-lost parents or grandparents – as if everything you've heard in your life, up till then, had just been an echo of something that all along had been planted right here. And the echoes of that something could still be heard…

Have you ever felt Patmos to be like one big monastery? The great Abbey of St. John, the first structure you see as your boat comes in, certainly sets a cloistered tone, and there are so many chapels here and church bells ringing. Just yesterday I saw a huge brass baptismal font sitting at the dock – now how often does one see that anywhere? And let's not forget that big blue neon cross over on the opposite mountain that lights up at night – I think you can see it from your porch!

Well, I guess you can make some associations there. The feeling of sanctuary is quite evident. But I think the island is simply a place where strangers may more easily become friends. It's interesting how when St. John came here, he emphasized the need to love. "Just love one another," he would say. So we are meant to form relationships, to network. One star can't illumine the whole night sky. Constellations have to form.

Patmos then seems to be a model for harmonious living, a kind of cosmic school of higher learning.

I do believe that very much – it's a wholesome place that naturally fosters self-discovery and genuine *agape*. There's a living tradition here. I felt a great wave of peace when I came to Patmos, and I still sense these peaceful rhythms. Things are free-flowing here. The sunlight writes on the water, and the waters wave in the light. Even the birds seem to fly in a more peaceful way, as if they know that they are loved. Animals are like children because they know when they are loved, and when they are not.

You live on an island that for centuries has been associated with the Apocalypse and the climax of human history. Do you feel that we are living in the last days?

It's funny how everyone is thinking about the last days with all the millennium hoopla, but I don't really dwell on that topic. I'd rather let everyone else focus on the subject. Anyway, every day is a dress rehearsal for the last day.

Did you ever want to go further East, into China? And what about Israel?

It's conceivable that if I had gone to Israel, I might have heard more ancestral voices, but I found so much here that I never truly experienced the impetus to go there.

As for the East, I think that may have become too artificial for me. My cultural roots lie in the Mediterranean world.

In a mystical sense, perhaps our psyches, our very genes, get most activated in and around those lands from where our blood lines come.

Yes, that could be.

Did any of your Columbia University friends come out here to visit you? Did they know where you went? I've read some early literature about Merton and Reinhardt and when your name came up, I found the line "Whereabouts unknown."

You're right. Many people thought the world had opened up and swallowed me. But my good friends knew of my whereabouts. Ed Rice came to visit. Merton intended to but never actually got here. Other old friends have come by over the years and we've had great conversations.

When you left the hustle and bustle of America and began a simple, eremitic life here in the Greek isles, I'm sure some of your friends in the States must have thought that you had made the wrong move. They had seen you launch on a promising career with various magazines such as Time *and* The New Yorker, *and then you suddenly gave it all up.*

Yes, I'm sure some people scratched their heads and wondered what I was up to, but I was simply being true to my own feelings.

Joseph Campbell used to say, "Follow your bliss."

That's right. It was something like that for me. All I can say is thank goodness I came out here, here by the sea.

Why do you find it necessary to live near the sea, whether in Marseille, Kalymnos, or Patmos?

I prefer to live near water, especially the sea, because it is one of the elements I like to be close to. If I'm inland somewhere, I usually find myself gravitating toward a river or such, but my mind inevitably goes to the sea.

What is it about the sea? Is it a spiritual metronome? A collective flow of universal consciousness?

That's interesting. It's the sound, the rhythm, the pulse, the light, the colour changes. Moment by moment the sea is never quite exactly the same, and yet it's still the sea, that is, you continue to recognize its greater form. And us old fellows, we know the sea's a lifegiver – we just smile and breathe her in.

You seem to go by various names on this sea-ringed place. I know your good buddies from America and Europe sometimes refer to you as Uncle Bobo, Robo, Sambo, Robo-Lax, and the like, but the islanders here hail you as "Petros."

Well, when I lived on the nearby isle of Kalymnos for some years they called me by my given name, "Roberto."

But later, when I came to Patmos and I told them who I was, they replied, "So your name is Petros?" I didn't argue.

The "Petros-Peter connection" is interesting. You live on a floating rock and you are something of a spiritual fisherman, which reminds me of St. Peter.

(Laughter). You can interpret anything, after a while.

Having finally settled on Patmos, were you ever fearful about what your future would be like here? Nobody knew you. It was a long way from New York. It must have been like starting all over again.

I suppose there were some times when I felt uneasy about things that were happening, but I didn't let these feelings keep me from believing that everything would turn out OK. The things I was unsure about just reinforced my listening. I listened more to myself and did the best that I could do in whatever situation I was faced with. I never lost faith. And I kept in mind the blessed peace I sensed when I first came.

Speaking of fearful moments, when you first came to the Greek isles you were accused of being a spy because all you seemed to do was walk around, observe the scene, and take notes. Then you would disappear into your house for long stretches of time. Of course, you were gathering creative material and writing, but that's not what they thought. The police even went so far as to interrupt your mail — they accused you of sending secret signals to the Turks! And this was during the "Reign of the Colonels" — a very sensitive time in the political and military history of modern Greece. Many natives were on the lookout for suspicious activity.

All of that is true.

Didn't that bother you? Weren't you nervous? How could you go on working in such a threatening environment?

Number one, I knew that I was not a spy, and I knew that God knew I was not a spy, no matter what they thought. But people are always apt to think of bizarre things, and that's what was happening then. Secondly, I felt it best to live here and endure periodic suspicion and all that funny stuff rather than go back to New York or anywhere else. To this day, I've never gotten tired of living here.

Years ago you told me that you moved quite a lot on Kalymnos and Patmos in search of adequate housing.

That's right. I did move many times.

Why all the moves? Sounds like tent city to me.

Moses or Heraclitus oughta answer that one! (Laughter). What did that pre-Socratic Heraclitus say? You can't step into the same river twice? Things are always on the move, changing, flowing. But to respond, a lot of things came into play. Convenience, making new friends, new areas of focus, better locale. And as far as cost goes, we're talking about the days when $50.00 might rent you a place for a year.

That's phenomenal! And all those moves…the whole thing sounds so nomadic. I do think of Moses and the wandering tribes, of caravans, gypsies, circuses…there's a lot there.

Yes, that's true. But in a more practical way, most of the moves had to do with living near town so I would not have to make extensive shopping trips. At the same time, I had to live in a distant place so I could write quietly, undisturbed. There was a good deal of hopping back and forth in the search for the right spot to live.

Did you work at odd jobs while you were writing?

No. I certainly helped people and volunteered my services when I could, but I can't remember having a paying job.

(In jest). But weren't you the captain of a big fishing vessel berthed at Patmos?

Nope, that's a legend that got started later and was based upon my stint at the wheel.

Are you serious? You piloted a ship?

You mean I never told you this story?

Please tell me now.

Well, one of the captains at the dock – I think his name was Christodoulos – he and I were going over to the isle of Lipsos on his big boat. We may have been bringing water bottles to the island. Anyway, he suddenly asked me to take over the helm, and he turned the wheel over to me. I was doing fine, so on the way back, he asked me to steer as well. But on the return trip, a little boat got in front of us.

Is that when you launched the torpedo?

(Laughter). No. But I quickly turned the wheel – as fast as a car driver trying to avoid something on the road might do. The ship kind of shuddered, and Captain Christodoulos quickly ran up and grabbed the wheel. My seamen's papers were immediately revoked.

You know, Bob, that can be interpreted as an allegorical lesson. If you try to jerk yourself out of a desperate situation in life, you might end up capsizing. But if you slowly, smoothly circumvent the problem, it's better for all.

Very true. Sounds like you're getting the feel of the flow.

We'll see. My voyage has just begun.

Alone with God

You call yourself a hermit, yet you have chosen to live near people. You periodically mingle with society. Why?

Most of my time is spent alone listening, writing, reflecting. I do need to be alone, undistracted, so that I can best hear myself think. Yet I've found that my solitary work, my writing and meditation, also comes to help out other people. So, in a sense, I'm not really alone even when I am alone, or, should I say, alone with God. Anyway, I'm not self-sufficient by any means, so I do go out into the world. And I like meeting people. But I also exercise my need for a solitary existence – I have always remained careful about that.

Have you ever felt lonely?

I can't say that I have. Yet I have had moments when I've asked myself, what am I doing here? Is it really me sitting here wishing to hear a voice? But no, no…I've never felt truly lonely.

Since you do spend most of your time alone, how do you keep up with what's happening beyond Patmos?

I get letters. I talk with people. My two dear nieces, Marcia and Connie,[22] keep me up-to-date. And ever since a friend gave me a radio, I listen to the BBC. Lots of nice programs there.

Have you ever felt like the desert father St. Anthony of Egypt? Like Anthony, you have tried to flee from the world, yet the world has followed after you. There are people who come to Patmos in the hope of seeing and meeting you. Numerous times tourists have come up to me and asked, "Who was that man I saw you walking with the other day? Was that Robert Lax?"

You know, Merton said at some point that it isn't good to try and live anonymously in a well-known holy place, something about how it's harder to live quietly among the people... In any case, visitors come here for all sorts of reasons, and if they happen to meet me, that's fine.

You've met so many people over the years. Have you ever felt a strong attraction for anyone in particular? Can you tell me if you have ever been in love with someone?

Well, there's a trick to that phrase, "in love." I do *love*, but I don't really think I have been in love.

Is there something mystical about this? It's said that highly spiritual, holy people can't feel comfortable if they are engaged in a relationship with one person because they lose track of the big picture. In other words, they can't focus their complete love on the whole of humanity.

No, I don't think that's the case with me. My nature is to be solitary. When I shared a room in the past, I hardly spoke to whoever was with me. It's just the way I am. Like I used to say to some of my friends, maybe I'm just "unicellular." (Laughter). Even as a child, when the girls and boys were playing house, I never felt like playing that game. But as far as the man–woman relationship goes, I think that's a very good way to learn about love. The purest way to be together is to have children and raise a family, all in a loving, patient way. And that love should never go away, nor should it be worn away by illusion and suspicion.

That's certainly a generative, procreative outlook.

Certainly. It's very natural for men and women to be fathers and mothers. The desire to have children is both a conscious and unconscious impulse. So when a man and woman meet, they should become a couple, an honest, loving couple, and they should try to become parents. But at the same time, the monk and the nun can also meet, and together create a spiritual birth. In both cases, I think the real desire is to nurture. Calling this impulse to come together as purely "sexual" is a misnomer, a tragic limiting. That the two sexes are attracted to each other is a healthy drive, and is nothing to be shameful about! But if this natural drive is not properly channelled, then a lot of tragedy can result. We are all given so much energy, and because we don't listen to what's out there, because we aren't relaxed enough and open our eyes to the big picture, we lose track of the flow.

You always give such good advice. Have you ever seen yourself as a sage who helps those who have lost their way? In this small, simple house do you consciously send out wholesome spiritual energy so as to help the world? Sometimes when I think of you living on Patmos, I imagine that you are awake in the midnight hour, praying for a world that has long since gone to sleep. You're the last man left standing.

Everything about that I understand except that last phrase – "last man left standing." I mean, there are many thousands of people around the world who are trying to do the right thing for themselves and for others. So many have received the inspiration to do good, loving things and glorify the Creator. Lots of folks are trying to hold together the world in their own way. It's not unusual.

Yes, but you are a role model, a hero for many who have come into your life.

Well, that's nice. I'm glad they like me.

You know, you never lose touch with your humility.

Gee, I certainly hope I don't... (Laughter).

Robert, you've lived almost ninety years.

I have? I'm not even 85, I think!

(Laughter). OK, you're right — let's just say you've been around for a while. Do you feel that you completely know yourself, or are you still trying to discover who you are?

Honestly, I'm far from knowing myself completely. I keep trying to learn more, I really do. It would be good if I could discover more. There's so much left to see and hear. I'm always listening to myself, looking within. I think that if we all try to discover more of ourselves, we can help each other out in the understanding of who we are, both as individuals and as a collective people. Every day I come to see what makes me more peaceful. If I can find this out for myself, maybe my quest can eventually help others. There are so many points of connection between people, so many original sights and sounds that we share, as if we were one creation but didn't really know it…but maybe we were meant to find out slowly.

Do you think that in the afterlife we will continue to find out more about who we are? Do you feel that when we've reached the last step and finally cross the bridge, we'll find more steps, more bridges?

Frankly, I must admit that I don't know. I've been letting the afterlife take care of itself, old man. But since God is infinite, then perhaps the journey to Him is, in actuality, a never-ending journey *through* Him, an eternal flow of increasing consciousness, at least on our part. Maybe if we shared more, we would know more.

That's something to think about. You know, you often emphasize the need for people to help each other. You've lived your entire life that way too. Yesterday I was talking to the grocer Panteli, your old friend in Skala, and he was telling me some stories about you, all good ones.

Well, I hope so. News travels fast on this rock.

He mentioned how you used to bring candles to a church named St. Evdokia for the congregation's use. He added that near the church lived a man named Damianos Theodosiou, a good friend of yours.

Oh, yes, Damianos the fisherman! We used to swim together down at the beach. That's where I met him. He also took me to various coastal areas of Patmos with his caique. We travelled to many coves and beaches. Truly, he's a very devout man who loves to do all he can for the churches near his home, particularly St. Evdokia, since his wife bears the name of the saint. There's a great story about him that the whole island knows.

Let's hear it.

Damianos was in the Merchant Marine earlier in life. At a certain point on a return trip from America, a big storm came up while he was on deck. A huge wave came crashing over the ship and threw him into the sea, and he thought he was finished. But what followed, though it sounds hard to believe, is that a second wave came, and brought him right back on deck.

Amazing! And this is a true story?

Absolutely. In fact, Ritsa, the wife of our artist friend Niko,[23] said that the same thing happened to her father. So perhaps it's not as unusual as one might believe.

Talk about salvation! Then again, perhaps they were so surprised, they had no time to be afraid and thrash about. They literally went with the flow, and the flow brought them back.

Good observation, Steve-O! If in the waters of life we relax, we float. If we struggle, we sink.

You know, I really find it interesting how you met Damianos at the beach, in an aqueous environment. You live surrounded by water. Many of your dream-visions, at least those that I've read, contain water imagery. Water has played an important part in your writing, swimming routine, and meditation. Your very idea of "flow" relates well with water. It all has a distinctly embryonic feel to it, as though you were perpetually being reborn in this fluid atmosphere.

That's quite true. As a matter of fact, almost everyone who swims in these waters comes out feeling reborn. The sensation is really there, of coming out of the womb again. I'm sure at least half of the locals could relate to that feeling of rebirth after coming out of the sea. It makes for a brand new beginning.

Wildflower

With regard to swimming and exercise, I know that keeping fit means a lot to you. You believe in preventative medicine and alternative therapies; you take vitamins and eat various health foods.

Speaking as one who is *monachos* (alone), if I don't try to take care of myself, things might become difficult. If I were unhealthy, that would probably affect my work and my ability to help those who happen to come my way.

That makes sense. What kinds of exercise have you engaged in over the years?

Swimming, of course. And many years ago a Chinese visitor advised that before I do anything else in the morning, I should walk a good clip for about forty minutes, especially up and down hills. So I would walk down the road to the sea and then come back, and I would keep on doing that until I was breathing deeply. I've gone up and down a lot of the hills of this isle.

"Yes, old boy, the important thing is to love – just love, love, love!" Lax conversing with the author inside the hermitage in the winter of 1999, less than a year before his passing.

"Dreams seem so much like pathways of light, like stars to steer by." The dreamcatcher in Lax's home.

The view out to sea from Lax's porch. A busy day for the island, as is evident by the many ships anchored in the bay. On the opposite mountain range is the Shrine of the Virgin of Koumana, where at night a large blue neon cross illuminates the evening sky.

"Bobcat" (Robert Lax) talking to a few of his "catkins" outside his hermitage.

"Petros" (Robert Lax) heads out toward a fishing boat that has just arrived in Skala.

A Patmian converses with Lax in the main square of Skala.

"And when you looked into the water, what did you see?" Lax and the author walk beside the Bay of Holaka, Patmos.

"Circus Roberto." Lax and the author clown around in the hermitage.

Have you ever stopped to consider that you were ahead of your time? Back in the early sixties you left an increasingly stressful "9 to 5 meat and potatoes TV-tuned America" and opted for a simple, organic, exercise-rich and creative lifestyle — everything the doctors are telling us to do now.

You know, I've never given that much thought. You're not gonna put me on a box of Wheaties, now are you? (Laughter). I was just doing what felt right and natural at the time. That's all I can say.

And your health routine also involves yoga, right? I'm sure your early interest in India pointed you in that direction.

Yes. But my exercises are essentially freestyle. I'm not bound to any system.

"To thine own self be true."

You betcha.

Did you take up any of the Chinese martial arts?

No, all of that swinging and kicking is not for me. I admire Tai Chi, but I never studied even that softer style.

Do you think that the regular exercise of your body, mind, and spirit over the years has helped you to evolve into a "young" octogenerian?

Well, if you think I'm still young, it's probably because I have no adult interests.

(Laughter). So you will always be a child chasing fireflies?

Maybe something like that. Why not?

What is your daily schedule like? What does it centre on? I know you get up at odd hours of the night and write by flashlight, but what is the whole routine like?

Every day I try to find out more about the spirit of peace within myself. Everything I do now, I try to relate it with that. Writing is my craft, and if I can in any way cultivate peace through it, then I'm happy. Lately it seems that no matter what I've been doing in the midnight hour, I'm up at 6 a.m. I do some breathing exercises, stretch a bit. I meditate for a while and read the Psalms. Those morning hours can be so peaceful. Before 12 I'm usually writing. Sometimes I levitate. (Laughter). Then if I'm up to it I go for a short walk outside here in cat alley, then do some things around the house. And I'm reading, reflecting throughout the day. I've been spending a lot of my time on my bed reading, writing, listening, dreaming…

Are you really happy now? You walk much less than you used to.

What do you want this old-timer to do, anyway? (Laughter). No, I really am happy, happy as can be. Sure, I'm not walking much now, but I get around. I just wish I could tell you how happy the dreams and things like that have been. That fine line between sleeping and waking is really beautiful. I really didn't know that things could be quite so wonderful, so peaceful like this – they really are nice. I've been writing poems on this.

As in your Sleeping, Waking[24] *collection?*

Yes, I'm writing more on that theme.

That sounds so encouraging. To be happy, creative, listening, loving, moving at an advanced age...

It *is* encouraging. That wonderful medieval artist and seer St. Hildegard of Bingen[25] and all her friends are right when they say to keep on moving in the right direction because you'll be glad when you do, as you do. So I keep on moving in the right direction. In my sleeping and waking I see good things happening.

And while you're at it, you're helping others along the path too.

Well, I'm just doing the best I can. Whatever it is I'm doing is all part of the flow. It's about rhythm and momentum, old man. Moving together forever.

What about the rhythm of eating? What kind of special diet do you follow? I know you like more healthy foods and drink a lot of water and grape juice.

I believe it is good to watch what you eat. For example, too much sugar and caffeine is not good for anybody. But let me first say that since youth I was more into vegetables just by nature. I simply prefer vegetables over meat. To think that some little creature had to die so I could eat him is painful for me.

Did Brahmachari influence you to eat more of a meatless diet?

Yes, surely there was that influence too. And in the *Book of Daniel*[26] there's that passage about the vegetarians being healthier than meat eaters. I think you told me about that when you were teaching that class – what was it?

99

Oh, yes, "Magic, Myth, Medicine," on ways of health in antiquity. But honestly, when I was young, my diet was based on pure folly. You see, I would routinely try to get the whole act of eating down to nothing so I could get on with my writing! So for weeks I might eat nothing but peanut butter or nothing but milk or yogurt – and that was because I didn't want to take time out to go to the store.

So you aren't perfect, after all!

Never said I was. I'm a wildflower!

(Laughter). Did asceticism have anything to do with your unconventional eating habits?

Not at all, my boy. It was pure laziness, that's all. Just getting the fuel intake down to zero. And there were other things, too. I never used condiments on my food. You might not believe it, but I never used salt till I was 28, and I stopped that pretty quick.

Well, the low salt intake was probably good for you. Anyway, you're so much different now. By that I mean that you take so much time whenever we eat together. You're so careful about what goes into a meal. You have rhythm, articulated movement. You pause often. Most of all, you say Grace.

Things happen along the way. But I've always been thankful for what I eat and for those who eat with me. And the health watchers are right when they say how you eat is just as important as what you eat.

I remember how before our meals, you would always invite me to say Grace. "Since God's the Giver," you'd say, "It's up to you to be the thanks-giver." You really liked one Grace-poem I composed — it used to be taped up there on your wall.

What did it say? Can you recall? When the postcards and art on my walls eventually fall down, I put up new things.

It was pretty simple. I think it went like this: Thank you for helping us to see how the flowers blooming here will bloom elsewhere. Nothing dies. For there is one Vine, one Root, one Stem. Whatever lives, will live again.

Yes, that was beautiful. I remember.

But Robo, there's one thing more I want to ask you about your diet, and that's your special fascination with yogurt.

Well, it's a cultured way of life that makes sense.

What, yogurt?

Steve, I thought you said yoga! (Laughter).

Well, I guess both yoga and the eating of yogurt together make for a cultured way of life.

Oh yes, certainly!

But what about yogurt? Your refrigerator is always stocked with it, and you're always offering me some topped with honey, not to mention the accompanying garlic pill.

Yogurt's marvellous, absolutely marvellous. It's a good, basic, simple food and yes, it's great with honey. About garlic, well, you know what they say about the powerful health effects of garlic. Lots of *whammo* there! (Laughter). And while we're at it, olive oil's fantastic too! You can't get enough of olive oil. But as for the yogurt, yeah, I've had quite a bit of that.

How many yogurts do you eat a day – four, maybe five?

I used to eat more. But the doctor who visits me every so often advised that I ease up on my intake, and I have. But it's so good. I think of it going deep down inside me and eradicating all those harmful microbes…

You're right. I just read an article on how science has proven that those live cultures in yogurt boost immunity. And being of Greek descent, I certainly have eaten a great deal of yogurt myself.

That's great to hear – glad to know we're both cultured! (Laughter).

Living in Grace

You travelled quite a bit in the States before heading out to Greece. Did you ever visit San Francisco? It was a formative literary and artistic city back in the fifties.

Yes, I was there briefly. That whole area is a lovely part of the world. I sure liked it a whole lot better than

Hollywood. San Francisco sort of reminded me of a European city.

Did you meet any San Francisco-based authors then? It was a formative literary time.

Let me think. I was there only a short while. Oh yes, I met Lawrence Ferlinghetti of City Lights Books.

How interesting! You know, a few months ago, an amazing thing happened. I went to a premiere showing of a documentary on the Beat Movement that aired at the Castro Theatre in the city. The movie's called The Source, *on Jack Kerouac, William Burroughs, and Lawrence Ferlinghetti. I was sitting there waiting for the program to start. The seat on my right was vacant. Just as the lights dimmed, who should take the seat but Ferlinghetti! We talked a bit, I brought up your name, and he remembered you.*

What did he say?

He wanted to know what you were doing out here. He knew that you had gone to Greece but never thought you'd be out here this long. In fact, he had wondered if you had gone on to the Happy Hunting Grounds!

My goodness, it's only been forty years. But really, Steve, that's a great story. You give my best to old Ferlinghetti, and tell him I'm still kickin' around.

All right, but can I ask you a more personal question?

All systems are go.

Are you afraid of death?

I've certainly thought about it. You know, a friend every so often sends me medallions of Our Lady of Mount Carmel. According to tradition, if you are wearing the medallion at the time of your passing, heavenward you go. But frankly, I'm too busy thinking about life to be meditating on death. I mean, when the time comes, we'll pick up our duds and return to where we came from. We're all brought into this life because heaven loves us, and back to that love we go. Now I know that death is certainly hard for those left behind. But tears are also part of the flow. Let them well up because they come as a blessing. It's the angels' way of helping to quiet the spirit so that prayers of love and hope may follow.

So what matters most is life. Live and let live.

No, cousin, it's more like live and *help live*. It's more like helping things to grow, even by a happy glance. It's about putting into practice every good thing you know. In doing this, you help out everyone, everything. And people are doing this all the time all over the world. I mean, if it wasn't for the help I've received from others, in many different places and situations, I may not have been here talking with you. You see, most of what I have – almost everything – has been given or sent to me by friends.

So you live explicitly on Grace, like Brahmachari.

Thank heaven it's true, so very, very, true. I think I've told you how over the years I have received things from different parts of the world, like Tokyo and New York, all on the same day, and the identical items were sent to me from both places. Sometimes they were things I needed at that moment, and there they were, in the mail, indicating that something good was going on...

Was it just coincidence?

Or Grace?

Or a "graceful coincidence"?

(Laughter). Yes, the same sort of thing happens with the postcards I get from around the globe, some of which are up there on my wall. There was a time when people from different places kept on sending me postcards of St. Jerome in his study, and they would arrive on the same day. And the strange thing is that I never gave too much thought to St. Jerome, that founding Latin father! But suddenly there he was with his books and astrolabe and hourglass, there he was in my mail and then up on my wall...

That must have been back in 1995. When we were on one of our meditative walks along the seashore, you asked me, "What does an hourglass mean to you?"

Yes, perhaps I did receive those St. Jerome cards during that time.

Speaking of St. Jerome, which Christian saints do you feel most close to?

Certainly St. Francis of Assisi, St. Hildegard of Bingen – now there's a good girl I like to chat with! Also the anchoress Julian of Norwich and the Russian Orthodox St. Seraphim of Sarov. And I really feel that Mother Teresa of Calcutta is the real thing, she truly is. I met her at a Catholic charity party. My feeling was that if you had to go anywhere and you wanted someone to take care of your kids while you were gone, she'd be the one. Compassionate, and with her feet on the ground.

I know you admire the religious classics of the East and West, but who are your favourite modern spiritual writers?

There are so many. Merton, of course, stands out. But others come to mind. Mircea Eliade, Teilhard de Chardin, Simone Weil, Bede Griffiths. Griffiths made an admirable effort in bridging the East and West.[27]

Can you tell me which authors and/or books have strongly influenced you?

Well, off the top of my head – and this may take a while – the Bible, most certainly. And Homer, Plato, Aristotle, St. Augustine, St. Thomas Aquinas, St. John of the Cross, Chaucer, Dante, Shakespeare, Rabelais, Pascal, Dumas, Blake, Swinburne, Thoreau, Emerson, Whitman, Ludwig Wittgenstein, Henri Bergson, Oscar Wilde, Joyce, Beckett …and, of course, there's all the Eastern literature.

I've always liked Kenko's *Tsurezuregusa* (Essays in Idleness), the Confucian anthology *Reflections on Things at Hand,* the Taoist writings of Lao Tzu and Chuang-Tzu, *The History of Chinese Philosophy* by Wing Tsit Chan, the Buddhist *Dhammapada, The Tibetan Book of the Great Liberation* as edited by Evans-Wentz, and of course, Merton's works which focus on the East. I've recommended a lot of these titles and authors to you in the past, I know.

What poets do you read, particularly modern poets?

Certainly T.S. Eliot, if that's what you mean by modern. Also Ezra Pound, Gertrude Stein, Wallace Stevens, Amy Lowell, Edna St. Vincent Millay. But the name that comes most clearly to me is William Carlos Williams. His words are so well chosen, so visual, so rhythmic and resonant. He has an economy of expression that is not tight-fisted. His words are liberating. He flows. He's musical.

I know that you also like the poetry of John Donne and Gerard Manley Hopkins. Why?

Hopkins is way up there, a real poet. His technique is admirable. Both Merton and I loved him. And we were also very fond of Donne. He's such a technically talented, assiduous poet. Besides that, his dedication to the Most High was the central aspect of his life. His dedication, his craft, his inner spiritual searching made him a wise man, so that by the time he committed his thoughts to writing, he clearly had something wonderful to say. Merton picked up a lot from him, particularly the idea that "No man is an island."

What are you reading lately?

Every day I try to read a number of authors, such as Matthew Fox, Hildegard of Bingen, Moses Maimonides. And I'm going through Merton's *The Way of Chuang Tzu*, Martin Buber's *Ten Rungs*, and Jean Vanier's *Meditations*. I also read from the Psalms daily – now there you'll find wonderful poetry. And I like reading books on the Jewish mystics and the Sufi mystics too. *Conference of the Birds* by Farid al-Din Attar, a Sufi sage, has been a favourite of mine. But in all my reading, I've learned that it's not how many books you read, but how well you know the choice few that are closest to your heart. However, to find out which books are dearest to you, you do have to play the field.

Do you have any ideas as to how one should go about reading? Is there any technique you advise?

Follow the practice that best suits you. But I've always believed that it's good to be calm before reading; deep, gentle breathing can help with this. And for the long haul, read carefully, perceptively, slowly, and in a gathered way, keeping in mind both the part and the whole of whatever it is you're focused on. Rushing a read is like rushing a meal!

That's for sure. Now aren't you also reading, as of late, the works of Eknath Easwaran, the well-known Indian scholar and follower of

Gandhi who did so much to popularize meditation and non-violence in America?

That's right. I just got through re-reading his advice on going slow, relaxing, focusing the attention, absorbing every word in the mind and heart, all the good things that make for centred living – wisdom which the ancients have intoned for centuries. His writings on daily meditation are great. You really ought to visit him out there in California. I think he lives somewhere near San Francisco.[28]

Robert, it seems that throughout your life, you have been an integrator, an ecumenical and interfaith thinker. In a sense, you foresaw the multicultural, interdisciplinary thrust that the world would take in the latter half of the twentieth century. You've seen how people have gradually felt the need to become interdependent and united in order to survive. You've been a harmonizer, a "world binder" since your days at Columbia, and you are among the last of your grand circle of creative and innovative comrades. Do you feel that you were anticipating the idea of a "global community," and sought to realize it through creativity, non-violence, and integrative thinking?

That's a mouthful! (Laughter). No, not really – nothing on that super scale. The only kid on the block I'm trying to integrate is my poor little old self. I mean, if the whole world disappeared tomorrow and I was left alone on a desert island with my pencil and notebook, I'd still go on trying to pull myself together and learn about who I am.

Given the chance, would you want to live another ninety or so years on earth, or would you rather go on to the next level?

If heaven would want me to live for another eight or nine decades, I'd be very happy to. But whatever happens, may it be according to the wishes of heaven. I go with the flow.

That sounds like a pretty tranquil philosophy.

And why not? I think it was the Taoists who said, "If you relax and make yourself comfortable, you can journey anywhere."

¹ Lax had always expressed an interest in dreams and dreaming. In his latter years, the practice of Tibetan dream yoga especially intrigued him. For more on this topic, see *Ancient Wisdom: Nyingma Teachings on Dream Yoga, Meditation, and Transformation*. Venerable Gyatrul Rinpoche. New York: Snow Lion, 1993. Merton was also fond of dreams, as demonstrated by his journal entries.

² See Carl Jung's *Dreams* and *Modern Man In Search Of A Soul*. Also of note is Jung's autobiography, *Memories, Dreams, Reflections*.

³ St. John of the Cross (1540–1591) was a Spanish Carmelite poet and mystic who believed that God is best found in remote, unlikely places and situations which impel the seeker to let go of the self and experience a higher, all-embracing reality. Like many mystics, such as St. Teresa of Avila, St. Francis of Assisi and St. Bonaventure, he felt that our deepest desires can only find complete fulfillment in God. His best-known works include *The Dark Night of the Soul, The Ascent of Mt. Carmel,* and *The Living Flame of Love.*

⁴ Father Ireneaus Herscher was the generous librarian at St. Bonaventure's Friedsam Library who granted Lax (and later Merton) extended borrowing privileges. Herscher was close to Lax and was instrumental in directing him to the Franciscan classics and other foundational texts of Christian mysticism. He would also become a spiritual mentor for the young Merton and is mentioned in *The Seven Storey Mountain.*

⁵ St. Thomas Aquinas (1225–1277) was a scholastic philosopher. He is best known for his encyclopedic-length works (*Summa Contra Gentiles, Summa Theologiae*) and for making the thought of Aristotle known and acceptable to the medieval Christian West. His sublime contemplation of the Deity and vast contributions to theology, metaphysics, psychology and moral philosophy earned him the title "The Angelic Doctor." It is highly interesting to note that shortly before his death, he experienced a mystical revelation which led him to say that his life's work seemed "like so much straw" in comparison to what had been supernaturally revealed to him. Perhaps it was for this reason that as Lax spiritually matured, he came to identify strongly with

St. Francis and St. John of the Cross, saints of poverty, kenotic spirituality, and emptiness who mystically and creatively emphasized the supremacy of love.

⁶ *The ABC's of Robert Lax,* 13. A letter Kerouac wrote to Lax may be found in *Jack Kerouac: Selected Letters 1940–1956.* Edited by Ann Charters. New York: Penguin, 1996, 446–448. Lax periodically wrote to Merton about Kerouac, as seen in his 1961–1964 letters (see *When Prophecy Still Had a Voice: The Letters of Thomas Merton and Robert Lax,* A. W. Biddle, ed. Lexington: University Press of Kentucky, 2001).

⁷ Edward Rice (1918–2001) died on August 18, nearly a year after his lifelong friend, Robert Lax, passed away. Rice, along with Lax and Merton, formed a close camaraderie at Columbia University and contributed to the campus publication *Jester* (Rice became Editor in Chief). After college, Rice founded the award-winning lay Catholic magazine *Jubilee* in 1953 and authored over twenty books, including a biography of his godson, Thomas Merton (*The Man in the Sycamore Tree,* New York: Doubleday, 1970). An acclaimed photographer and artist, Rice, like Lax, was a friend of Ad Reinhardt, a fellow student at Columbia and a staff member of *Jester.*

⁸ The Monastery of St. John, located in the high town of Hora, remains the great Byzantine bastion of Patmos, and is visible from many parts of the isle. Its massive foundations were laid in 1088 under the direction of Christodoulos the Wonderworker, a monk who was later canonized. The castle-like labyrinthian structure is especially famous for its library, archives, and treasury which contain priceless manuscripts, icons, and holy relics.

⁹ Merton wrote a humorous poem about Lax's brief film stint. See *A Catch of Anti-letters.* Thomas Merton, ed. Kansas City, MO: Sheed & Ward, 1978, 127–128.

¹⁰ Jiddu Krishnamurti (1895–1986). Indian spiritual leader. While only a boy, he was proclaimed by Annie Besant, the International President of the Theosophical Society, to be the "World Teacher and Master" who would illuminate humanity (for more on Theosophy, see the following note). From 1909, Krishnamurti was raised and supported

by an elect circle of upper-class English and American Theosophists. An organization termed "The Order of the Star of the East" was soon after formed to promote Krishnamurti's development as "World Illuminator." However, Krishnamurti himself later repudiated this role and disbanded the Order. He attained fame as an eclectic teacher of Indian philosophy and mysticism and advocated that life be lived free from the confines of nationality, race and religion.

[11] Madame Helena Blavatsky was the champion of Theosophy ("Divine Wisdom"), a spiritual movement which originated in the late nineteenth century. Blavatsky sought to enhance the awareness between nature and spirit in order to achieve direct, intuitive knowledge of the divine. Theosophy integrates the currents of Neoplatonism, Gnosticism, Alchemy, Kabbalism, Buddhism, and Hinduism. The primary tenets of the faith emphasize four points: the spiritual investigation of the universe, the development of the psychic powers of humanity, the rediscovery of the secret and esoteric teachings of ancient religions and divine masters (particularly as found in Eastern belief systems), and the unity of the "brotherhood of man," as exemplified in the presumed "oneness" of all religions. The classic foundations of Theosophy may be found in Blavatsky's *The Secret Doctrine* (1888).

[12] Mark Van Doren, Professor of English Literature at Columbia University, was a teacher and friend to both Lax and Merton. Of Lax, Van Doren wrote that he was filled with "A sort of bliss that he could do nothing about... Lax could not state his bliss, his love of the world and all things and persons in it" (*The ABC's of Robert Lax*. Edited by Miller and Zurbrugg. London: Stride, 1999, 190).

[13] Jacques Barzun taught history for fifty years at Columbia University and was Lax's faculty advisor. He was a founder of the discipline of Cultural History at Columbia and led seminars with Lionel Trilling that were famous for their style, wit and substance. The author of more than thirty books, his most recent publication, completed at the age of 92, is *From Dawn to Decadence,* an 800-page study which focuses on a series of socio-political-religious ideas that have evolved in Western History over the past 500 years.

[14] Ad Reinhardt (1913–1968) was a close classmate of both Lax and Merton at Columbia University and would later become a leading member of the American Abstract Art movement. Like many of the Abstract Expressionists, Reinhardt was influenced by Eastern art and philosophy. His final style was typified by a five foot square canvas divided into nine equal sections, each of which was painted black. Interestingly, what emerges from this apparently monochrome canvas is a cross-like structure. Reinhardt is discussed at length in *"Art,"* the third dialogue section of this book.

[15] Dorothy Day (1897–1980). Born in New York, she was a social reformer and writer. Day converted to Catholicism in 1927 and founded the "Catholic Worker Movement" which established "Houses of Hospitality" during the Great Depression. A profound pacifist, Day helped to turn the Church's attention to peace, justice, and homelessness issues. Lax, in his youth, read poetry in her New York apartment where artists and thinkers periodically gathered. Her autobiography, *The Long Loneliness,* was published in 1952. In her later years, she is said to have imbued a prayerful aura of holiness.

[16] Jacques Maritain (1882–1973). Born in Paris, Maritain, a Protestant, converted to Catholicism in 1906 and became a world-renowned professor of theology, teaching in Europe, Canada, and America. He also served as French Ambassdor to the Vatican. Maritain's writings on art and philosophy, especially his work on Thomas Aquinas' theory of knowledge and its modern applications, influenced both Lax and Merton.

[17] From his early twenties, the acclaimed Canadian Jean Vanier has been an advocate for the disadvantaged and disabled. Born in 1928, he went on to found L'Arche in 1963. This is the community that subsequently became the basis for a worldwide organization which builds ecumenical centres for the handicapped and those workers who assist them. Vanier, a past professor at the University of Toronto, is a philosopher and theologian who in his youth was deeply influenced by reading Thomas Merton's *The Seven Storey Mountain.* Vanier is himself a best-selling author whose beliefs may be read in such publications as *An Ark for the Poor, The Heart of L'Arche, Our Journey Home* and *The*

Scandal of Service – published by Novalis – and *Becoming Human*, published by Anansi in Canada and Paulist Press in the U.S.

[18] The eminent Hindu monk and theologian, Dr. Mahanambrato Brahmachari, had died on October 18, 1999, the day I left San Francisco for Patmos and met with Lax a final time. Both Lax and I were unaware of his passing. Brahmachari arrived penniless in America in 1933, sent by his monastery to attend the Conference of World Fellowship of Faiths. His trust in divine grace, that God would take care of him in any situation, gave him the fortitude to live, learn, and teach in America from 1933–1939. During this time, he received many honours from American and international theologians.

[19] For Lax's Marseille experiences, see "Port City: The Marseilles Diaries" in *Love Had A Compass*. Edited by James Uebbing. New York: Grove Press, 1996.

[20] Padre Pio (Francis Forgione, 1887–1968) is the famous Franciscan mystic of the Capuchin order. Many miracles, both during and after his life, have been attributed to him. Perhaps the most famous attributes of Padre Pio were his stigmata (he bled daily for fifty years) and his reputed ability to bilocate. Father Pio's following is great, especially in his native Italy. For more on this stigmatic and miraculous phenomena associated with him, see *The Sanctified Body: An Expert On 19th and 20th Century Holiness Looks At Levitation-Bilocation-Perfumes of Sanctity-Supernatural Energy-Human Luminosity.* Patricia Treece. New York: Doubleday, 1989.

[21] The Cave of St. John remains the most holy site on Patmos. The grotto marks the place where, according to early Church tradition, St. John the Evangelist and Disciple received the *Revelation* from Jesus Christ. The cave gave shelter to the elderly St. John who was banished to Patmos by the Roman Emperor Domitian in 95 AD (the isle then served as a penal colony). Many miracles are said to have transpired at the cave and continue to this day. The islanders attribute much of this supernatural activity to St. John, who functions as the protector of Patmos.

[22] Marcia Kelly and Connie Brothers, the daughters of Benjamin and Gladys Marcus, were close to their uncle throughout his life and regularly looked after his health and general well-being.

23 Niko and Ritsa Eliou are artists who live on Patmos. They were close friends of Lax. Niko is a painter and poet. Ritsa is a potter and ceramic artist.

24 *Sleeping, Waking* by Robert Lax, 1997, is a limited edition work (75 copies) selected and arranged by John Beer, friend and editorial assistant of Lax.

25 Hildegard of Bingen was a thirteenth-century German abbess famous for her artistic and literary gifts, prophetic ability, expertise in science and healing, and dynamic reform movements. She believed that the world is composed of interrelated hierarchical states set into effect by the Creator which on no account should be disturbed but carefully nurtured. In 1165, she founded a convent in Eibingen, near the Rhine, which in the twentieth century became the centre of the Hildegardian revival.

26 Daniel 1.8-16.

27 Father Bede (Alan) Griffiths, later to be known as Swami Dhayananda, was born on Walton-on-Thames in England in 1906. He received his education at Oxford in English Literature and Philosophy and was tutored there by C.S. Lewis, with whom he formed a close friendship. Shortly after his graduation, he converted to Roman Catholicism and entered the Abbey of Prinknash where he took the name of Bede. In 1955, he journeyed to India and assisted in the foundation of Kurisumala Ashram (The Mountain of the Cross), a monastery of the Syrian rite. In establishing this Christian ashram, Fr. Bede took the Sanskrit name Dhayananda. At Kurisumala (and later at the Saccidananda Ashram, founded in 1950 by Abbot Jules Monchanin and Henri le Saux), Fr. Bede's primary work lay in establishing interfaith dialogue between Christian and Hindu theology. Known for his compassion and gentleness, he was also a prolific author and is best known for *The Marriage of East and West* and *The Golden String*. He died in his hut at Shantivanam, in South India, in 1993.

28 Eknath Easwaran, founder and director of the Blue Mountain Meditation Center in Tomales, California, had died on October 26, 1999. Both Lax and I were unaware of his passing.

CRAFT

It is like a wind that surrounds me
Or a dark cloud,
And I am in it.
And it belongs to me
and it gives me the power
to do these things.

Robert Lax,
from *Circus of the Sun*

In examining Lax's many writings, a unifying theme emerges which reveals more about this eremitical spiritual poet – the theme of the circus. In 1949, Lax went on the road with the Cristiani Family Circus and afterwards produced his highly acclaimed poem-cycle, *Circus of the Sun*. While describing the drama and wonder of the "big tent," Lax compares the travelling circus with the world, itself a collective "megashow" spinning through space.

> I have often thought how much like the circus
> the world is, and how the more like a circus it
> becomes, the better...
> The traveling circus is always in motion. "Put it
> up and tear it down" is the constant chant of the
> circus...
> Like civilizations and everything that grows, it
> holds its perfection for but a little moment...
>
> Robert Lax, *Mogador's Book*, 14.

Lax faintly echoes St. Paul, who exclaimed how all things are continually in a state of flow and transition as the whole of life courses toward the Origin and End-Point of the cosmos: "For here we have no lasting city, but we seek the city which is to come.... For we know that if the earthly tent we live in is to be destroyed, we have a building from God, a house not made with human hands, eternal in the heavens" (Hebrews 13.14; 2 Corinthians 5.1). As Lax intones, we are all performers in the temporal "circus of life." Things of a day, co-participants of a universal dream, we wander gypsy-like through space. And though we may enthrall, amuse, and applaud one another as we journey toward our everlasting home, our chief audience is the almighty Ringmaster, the invisible "Sun" Who, like the light streaming in from the circular, wide-open tent top, illuminates our acts and moves with us in our lifelong performances. Rejoicing in our joy, raising us up should we fall, the Lord leads His circus according to His death-defying, rejuvenating Love.

In the *Circus of the Sun*, Lax describes a day in the life of a circus, beginning with the raising of the show tent at dawn and closing with its disassembly at dusk. In the process, he allegorically suggests that the passing of each earthly day is a cosmic circus in itself, designed and orchestrated by God. And if the great purpose of life, according to Lax, is to celebrate the Creator and unite with Him, then everyone is required to discover their God-given gifts, that through their lifelong implementation, they might draw near to the Almighty.

Both in life and in the circus, people are called to exercise their talents in a singular and universal fashion. While an individual may momentarily command the spotlight, all participants inevitably work together for the show to go on. As Lax relates, "Everyone who travels with the circus is of use to the circus. Nobody is just along for the ride" (Lax. *Mogador's Book*. 18).

Ultimately, the travelling circus spreads joy throughout the world. United, the many members of the troupe work in harmony, transmitting the "Good News" of wonder and happiness everywhere.

Our dreams have tamed the lions,
Have made pathways in the jungle,
Peaceful lakes; they have built new
Edens ever-sweet and ever-changing.
By day from town to town we carry
Eden in our tents and bring its wonders
To the children who have lost their dream of home.

Robert Lax,
Circus of the Sun

Marking Stones

When did you first realize that you would become a writer?

Very early, I believe. Writing has always made me feel comfortable, and at home. I remember making marks on stones as a child and expecting people to find my messages. The poetry came when I was about eight. My first poem was published when I was ten or so, and I decided to become a writer when I was fifteen. And being the kind of person who liked to hear advice, I was influenced by my sister Gladys, who encouraged my creative and literary interests. She impressed upon me how the writer is his own person and can travel anywhere. She knew my character well enough to know what would be good for me.

"Be truthful to thyself."

There's that old refrain again. (Laughter). So yes, I decided to become a writer, but exactly what kind of writer – that took me a while to find out. As a young man, I was seeing Eugene O'Neill and Noel Coward plays in New York, and at first thought that writing for the theatre would be a good thing. But after hanging around theatres for a while and being part of that crowd, I realized that I just couldn't write the way I wanted to if I was in an atmosphere like that.

Sort of like the later Hollywood experience.

That's right. My playwriting career was short-lived, you might say.

But your interest in acting and entertainment seemed to continue. You would later follow travelling circuses in America and Europe in which you participated as a clown, and you even played a part in a film shot in Greece. And some of your poems, like "The Bomb,"[1] are meant to be performed onstage.

That's true. But I guess it was all part of the path for me, a way of listening, a way of understanding what I was really trying to say. While I was in theatre and later in Hollywood, there seemed to be indications that the entertainment world was where I was supposed to be at the time. Merton had also pointed this out to me. That's why it's good to relax and let things flow – eventually things go where they are meant to. You really can't find out who you are if someone or something is incessantly trying to tell you what to do. Even truth, coming from a domineering voice, may sound like falsehood. That's why I like the "still small voice."

Me too. Dawn and dusk don't come all at once.

Thank heaven!

Earlier today I saw you writing in Greek, and I wanted to know when you learned the language. Was it on the Greek isles?

Yes, I began working on it when I was over here.

Do you write poetry in Greek?

No, although sometimes a Greek word fits in well with what I'm saying, so I use it and usually give a consequent translation.

Have your poems been translated into Greek?

Yes, but only a few, such as *Fables*, translated by my old friend Moschos Lagouvardos.[2] He's written a number of books and is a fine photographer.

Robert, from time to time, I've heard you mention Father Philotheus Boehner[3] when discussing your writing.

Sure, he was my spiritual advisor until I left for Europe. I chose him and trusted him. He was another mentor for me. He was also Merton's spiritual advisor when Merton was at St. Bonaventure University. I think he's mentioned in *The Seven Storey Mountain.* Father Boehner encouraged Merton to enter the Monastery of Gethsemani.

How exactly did he help you with your work?

Well, he gave good advice in many areas, including the arts. He understood the type of regimen an artist should set for himself. Father Philotheus suggested that the way to engage in writing, painting, or any art or discipline, is to go to the special place that you have selected for your work and remain there from a set time to a set time. The artist should do this every day, even if the juices aren't flowing. In the long run, the rhythm of the routine will work, and the creativity will flow. My friend Ad Reinhardt had the same philosophy. He didn't break that rule because he knew that the mind and body respond to rhythm. Eventually something automatic sets in. A voice inside says, "Here I am. Now I can start creating." It was just such a place I was looking for when I was making all those moves on Kalymnos and Patmos. I was looking for my "writing house" where each day I could stay for a particular time and write in peace. And I did get things written that I'm glad about.

What else do you remember about Father Philotheus?

Well, I do remember how when I was called upon to go on a trip to Europe for the Holy Year, he told me that

I should indeed go, but to come right back when it was over and get to work again. But by the time I got back, he had died. I had other spiritual advisors after him, some of whom were helpful in other ways as well. One was kind enough to forward my mail to the U.S. Embassy at Marseille when I was living there for a time.

When you were in France, who was your spiritual advisor?

A Carmelite priest. I can't remember his name now, but one day I came to him with a dilemma. I had twenty things I wanted to do. I was thinking of living in a cave with the Little Brothers of Jesus somewhere in the south of France. I was contemplating entering Eau Vive, a Dominican community in the north of France. There were so many paths to take, and I didn't know which one to choose. And then this priest drew a circle for me, sectioned it out like a pie, and said, "This is what you will do. The first three weeks you will go here, the next three weeks you will go there, and so on. You will explore all your interests according to a rhythm and program that makes sense." I could see how wise he was, how right he was because at that time I could never have come up with the calm, sweet idea of simply doing one thing at a time. I was too close to the forest, as they say. Anyway, I was beginning to sample pieces of that metaphysical pie when Ed Rice, editor of *Jubilee*, telegraphed me to come back to New York.

When you were working at Jubilee, you met Emil Antonucci,[4] one of your early illustrators and publishers. How did that happen?

Emil was a contributor and artist at *Jubilee*. As soon as we met, we hit it off just fine. He showed me some of his drawings, and I liked them. We got the idea that we could work together. So he began illustrating some of my poems, and he did so beautifully. What he liked in my writing was the minimalism and repetition, like "One stone, one stone, one stone…" He really dug that kind of expression, perhaps more so than anyone else. I think he saw that minimalism was a focus on the pure and absolute essentials – in a way like moving toward the four basic elements which, in turn, move back to a cosmic and divine origin.

Didn't you and he collaborate on various avant-garde film projects, like your New Poems *series?*

Sure, we did short films. I've always liked films ever since those days when I was watching Charlie Chaplin and Buster Keaton do their thing. But with Antonucci, it all started, I think, when I was alone in the office at *Jubilee* and was writing in my poem-journal. One of the things I wrote about was the action taking place out in the street, right across from my window at 27th Avenue and 4th. People were always passing in front of a bank, and I would take note of what was going on. One person consistently crossed himself as he went by the bank, as though he were going past a church. A few women always strode by as though they were storm troopers. And another man looked like he had a gun in his pocket because one arm was always tucked into his suit. Only later did I realize that the poor man had only one arm, and I reproached myself for that! Anyway, I had finished writing my observations, gave them to Antonucci to read, and he said, "Next Saturday, let's take a movie camera up to that same window and see what we get on film." The curious thing was that all the characters I had written about showed up, as if the entire cast had been summoned. We liked the results and did the same sort of thing in Harlem from a window in Friendship House. Later on, we also filmed in Washington Square Park. Lots of people who knew us came by, like the artist Bob Kagnowski[5], just in time to be in the movie.

So you have collaborated with other artists through the years?

Not particularly, but it's good to do that. You see new things, new possibilities. It's good to share. Artist colonies can be fun places.

What about poetry readings? Have you made it a point to read your works in public?

On rare occasions I have returned to the USA and read at Harvard, the University of South Dakota, and in the New York area. But most of my readings have been in Europe: in Zurich, Geneva, Florence. And I have done poetry readings and programs on European radio. Hartmut Geerken of *Bayerischer Rundfunk* in Munich has arranged many of these.

Have any of these readings ever integrated the works of Merton?

No, I don't think so.

You spent much time with Merton. Did he have any influence on your writing?

I wouldn't know exactly how he influenced me. Just being in his company was an influence! He handled the English language so beautifully. His vocabulary was much broader than mine. He was such an excellent writer. Anyone who is a good constructor of sentences is a teacher for me.

Which of his books do you like best?

One of my very favourites is *Mystics and Zen Masters*. And I also like *Seeds of Contemplation* and *Thoughts in Solitude*. His journal writing is also excellent – that collection titled *The Intimate Merton* is simply wonderful. He wrote so much, he was such an interfaith thinker and promoter of peace. Everything he has done is splendid. You can't get too much of Merton.

One of the Taoist stories Merton writes of has to do with the butcher whose knife never grows dull, no matter how often he uses it.[6] The explanation given is that he knows where to cut. He knows the spaces that exist between the joints, so his knife never has to force itself through anything. What do you think the story suggests?

It's about diligent practice as one travels the path of least resistance. The butcher is going with the flow, so he isn't fixated, dulled. Through his own value of empty space – that space from which all potentialities arise and which many people seem to ignore – he can perceive where lie the secret spaces in all of life, those quiet, open spaces that make everything else possible. So if you go with the flow, you intuitively know where to go, and you don't get worn away.

That's fascinating. Do you know that physicists say that 75 per cent of the universe is essentially pure space?

Space is certainly fundamental to the cosmos. There are spaces between musical notes and sounds, atoms and cells, even between universes, from what I've heard. Without it, creation just wouldn't make much sense.

Sacred Space

Most of your poems are not only minimalist in form, but at the same time exhibit radical spacing. What do all those spaces mean?

Well, I guess by pondering those spaces, you may find out. (Laughter).

Do you know that Merton wrote something like, "To know Bob Lax's writing, you really have to know what's in all the empty spaces"? What's in all those spaces?

No answer rushes to mind.

Empty space?

Empty space.

128

This talk of "empty space" is definitively Eastern in nature. Have you consciously tried to integrate elements of Asian spirituality into your verse?

No, I don't think I've consciously tried to do that, but subconsciously I think it's possible.

Did you steer Merton toward Eastern spirituality or did he influence you in this area?

That's a good question. Well, he did not have to introduce me to Asian mysticism because I had the Theosophical influence through my Uncle Harry. But I remember that conversation with Merton, I guess it was going up to Olean just after graduating from Columbia. I was talking about Mortimer Adler's writings on Catholicism, and even at that point Merton expressed a simultaneous interest in Buddhism. Certainly he had studied introductory concepts of Asian mysticism at Columbia and very much liked the wisdom of the East.

And since you and Merton helped to secretly house Brahmachari at Columbia, the Eastern influence was always there.

It was always there, and it was for Rice too. I mean, if we weren't living here in America, most of us would, I believe, wish to live in India. That was in all of us when we were young. And I think Ed Rice had a relative who had been out to India, so the attractiveness of the East was knitted into our group.

Your writing is getting better known in the States, but it has taken a while. In The New York Times Review of Books, *Richard Kostelanetz states that you are one of America's greatest experimental poets working in the minimalist style — that you remain the last unacknowledged major poet of the post-sixties generation.*[7]

Denise Levertov[8] and others have expressed similar sentiments. But I'm not in any rush to be recognized. Laying low helps. Fewer distractions. Really, it doesn't bother me.

But don't you think you deserve far greater recognition than you have received thus far? This also applies to areas other than writing. In your Columbia days, you were the one who organized many creative activities in which your friends participated, such as the novel-writing contests. And the "arts cottage" at Olean[9] *was supplied by you, courtesy of Benjamin Marcus, your brother-in-law. Not just this, but your influence on Merton — who considered you the "wisest of all" — is inestimable. You consistently encouraged him along his spiritual path, both verbally and in writing. Without you, there may never have been a Merton as we know him.*

Looks like you've done some homework. But like I said, it's not my nature to seek attention. And really, Merton and I influenced each other. It wasn't a one-way friendship. We sharpened each other's wits.

I see. What more can you say about your reductionist approach to writing?

I don't know… I do think of my work as minimalist. I also like to think of my work as abstract.

In your "abstract-minimalist" style you might create an entire poem based upon the words "black" and "white." What exactly do black and white mean to you? Does black designate what is "apophatic," and white symbolize what is "cataphatic"? Are you suggesting the "Yin" and the "Yang" here?

Well, I see black and white as two basic "building block colours" of the universe, just like night and day. If you're going to make a line on a white wall, the simplest colour to use would be black. And you also say things like, "Plain as black and white." Granted, a "black-white poem" may have greater mystical meaning, but any in-depth analysis of the verse is not required. It may sound elementary, but I simply like black and white. If others see more, that's great.

Don't you want your readers to see many meanings in your verse?

I don't know about *wanting*, but you certainly allow them to. Nobody's raising a sign that reads, "Prepare for the mystical overtones." I mean, some things are as plain and simple as a tree giving forth its fruit, or the sun giving light to the sky. It's up to the individual if deeper things are to enter the picture.

You mean the verse.

(Laughter). You know what I mean.

Exactly what prompted you to write minimalist poetry?

Certainly wordiness never had a good name in the trade. With regard to literary influences, Haiku showed me how minimal text can have maximum effect. And I was very much moved by James Joyce. *Finnegan's Wake* was really an eye-opener. A certain flow was there. Joyce said something about the economy of verse which really meant a lot to me. He said, "Write as though you were sending a telegram, and each word costs so much." This was exciting, yet while I began to condense my verse, I made a conscious effort not to eliminate its rhythm, imagery, and music.

What was it about this abstraction process that appealed to you?

Abstraction means cutting down to the essentials. New things therefore became possible. For instance, if I write "blue sea," I've limited what blue can refer to. But if I simply write "blue," blue can be the sea, the sky, an emotion, all kinds of things. Writing in an abstract mode is liberating.

I see in your attempts to condense everything into a single liberating word something of a creative "big bang" — each meticulously crafted word is like a seed which you gently plant in the mindscape of the reader, and in the reader everything is meant to flower.

Oh, that's beautiful, Steve-O.

Truly, your minimalist poems demonstrate how words are launching points into the realm of the heart. In a humble way, they don't attract attention to themselves. They open a door through which the reader passes.

Well, that's really a kind analysis.

Yeah, I think it sounded pretty cool myself, Bob.

Like real super neat-o?

Wow, what a hip expression! Hail the born-free Robo-Lax!

Pow! Wham! Zowie!

(Laughter). What can I say? I think we just had something of an "Anti-letter experience"![10] But tell me, as you write your sparse, concentrated verse — say you write "river" ten times over — what goes on in your mind?

I guess the word itself and its meaning. And I'm interested in the syllable structure of the words, their placement, their rhythm, their interrelationship, how they play against each other. For instance, "Red Red Red" has a different effect than "Blue Blue Red."

That sequencing sounds a bit like DNA coding.

Yes, you can make that type of association.

As you write "river," do you feel the flow of the water? Are you trying to project the reality of the watercourse into your verse?

Well, as I write the word, I certainly feel what a river means. That's how I know what the word itself calls to mind, what it invokes and expresses in its purest form. But subconsciously I might be thinking of a stream of consciousness or a stream of creativity whose source is the Creator.

In being so economical with your verse, I get the sense that you don't want to put any words down that you don't intrinsically feel. Whatever you write you are comfortable with because you "walk your talk," you live your words.

That's true. You should choose words that mean something to you, that you can truly identify with, especially when writing in the minimalist mode. So you concentrate your focus. It's a refining process, and it's about a kind of musical resonance too. I mean, it's good to make the harmonies happen in such a way that you don't do anything too forcefully, too possessively, as though you were trying to say it all — nobody can do that, anyway. Just let expression come naturally. And like they say in the East, things have meaning outside the labels or descriptions you might give them. We've got to be conscious of that space. So words should not really be endpoints, but work best as doorways to understanding.

Yes, I can really empathize with that. And what about the extensive repetition in your writing? Does it suggest the creative repetition inherent in the cosmos, as in the ceaseless wave action of the sea, the day-night sequence, the cyclic seasons?

Certainly all of that may be implied. I believe we're a part of this universal rhythmic process because we're all a part of nature — we are in it and of it. So like the ingoing and outgoing waves, we breathe in a similar way — we flow. Cosmic creativity and creative evolution are always going on. Everything is always singing.

At this point, can you relate how kenosis, or "mystical emptying," plays a part in your abstract and minimalist writing?

Now that's a big question. Figuratively speaking, kenosis has to do with the idea that when you give, you let go, you empty yourself, and as you do so, you place yourself in the position to receive more. It's cyclic, much like our breathing – you exhale, or give out, then you inhale, and take in. Giving-receiving; receiving-giving. I can't receive anything from nature if I've evaporated the sea with a burst of white-hot words. But with one cool little drop of a word there's plenty of room to reflect. The whole thing to do is to refrain from blocking the flow. In the kenotic mode, any trace of ego disappears right into what you are doing. You don't struggle with it anymore because you become an open door, a channel, a conduit. Like I've said, an unobstructed garden hose is a clear channel – it just does its work.

Does your kenotic "less is more" script reflect the pact you made with Merton in your college days, to "live simply and write simply"?

I believe it may have something to do with that. I have tried to live focusing on what is essential. When life is uncluttered, when verse is uncluttered, there is a greater freedom of movement and clearer vision. As they say, when the water is still, you can see right down to the bottom. We all pay homage to clarity.

What exactly is transmitted in language? There's the word, the rhythm of the word, the sound, the intonation, the meaning, but is there something more? Something spiritual, non-cerebral?

(Laughter). Why do you ask such complex questions? I think what is transmitted in language is pure and simple *communication*, the ability for one of us creatures to clearly communicate with the other. Yes, there is a spiritual component to everything we do, but I let heaven take care of that.

But aren't your minimalist poems springboards to something else? Chuang-Tzu said that the purpose of the fish trap is to catch fish; when the fish are caught, the trap is put away. So when the words have conveyed their meaning, are the words discarded? In your reductionist script, are you intimating wordlessness? Can language be a veil that obscures primal, intuitive meaning?

Sure. I think there's something to that. Language isn't an end in itself, but may suggest the presence of a greater reality in which all things are participating. But at the same time, sometimes you need the words to remind you of where you are headed, where you are going. If you lose your bearings, words can function like a compass and put you back on course. You stay on track.

So we should be sure to use our "verbal compass" from time to time?

Righto! Full speed ahead.

(Laughter). Aye-Aye, Captain.

Breathing, Writing

Do you write to make the world a better place?

First of all, I write to better understand myself and my relationship with everything else. If my writing does indeed influence the world in a positive way, either now or in some future time, I'm all for it. And if for some reason it doesn't, I'm OK with that too. But before any greater analysis is made, it's important to keep in mind that my work helps me to understand who I am. What happens after simply happens.

So when you write, you don't consciously try to enlighten the reader?

Not really. I simply trust that if my writing is meant to help out the reader, he or she will pick up on it. But if I sense that my words may hurt somebody or upset them, I won't write them.

How do you write? Do you compose best in the morning? Is there a special part of the day you set aside for writing?

I find that I write throughout the day and night. I do like writing by flashlight in the early morning hours, but there's no particular magic time. It's a process that always goes on consciously and subconsciously. It's all a matter of rhythm and flow. I write like I breathe, and I breathe like I write.

Why is breath so important in your writing?

Well, I guess it's important in living too. (Laughter). It helps us to pause, reflect, space things out. It's all part of the pulse and flow. The waves go in, the waves go out. Having some familiarity with surfing, you should know about this. Yes, we can learn a lot by looking at how we breathe.

Do you write with any pre-existent plan in mind?

I can't say I do. It's a matter of momentum and with what's there at the moment of creation. Poems come and go like the dreams that flow. What's important, though, is to have vision, to keep the vision clear. We were made to see both near and far.

Do you revise much?

Hardly. I think that if poetry is life and art is life – and I do – then I'm always focused on my craft. When the words come, I trust that they are the right ones.

So life is like one big poem?

A poem, a dream…we are moving through a sea of consciousness, a flowing dream.

Therefore your writing may be likened to revelation? A bit of light breaks through the dark, making the dream more tangible?

You might say that. But I think that in everything we do, we are revealing something to ourselves and eventually to others.

You know, the fact that you don't really revise reminds me of how the ancients treated their oracles.

What was that?

When inspired priests and priestesses received insights from heaven, they spoke aloud, and their words were recorded by scribes. These pronouncements were not tampered with because the words were considered holy, having come from beyond.

Oh, I like that…but please don't think I'm prophetic. (Laughter).

Whatever you say. But you seem to be ready for inspiration or at least dictation because you always carry a little notebook with you everywhere you go.

Sure, things pop into my head from time to time. Sometimes the right words do come up by themselves.

Do you make use of all your reflections?

Inevitably, I think everything becomes useful.

What does the word "poet" mean to you?

Creator…peacemaker…I'm also thinking about light, life, freedom, vision, spirit, song. Poetry is about song. That's really where language may have evolved from. People saw how beautiful that first garden was, and they sang. Then language – I mean communicating in an ordinary, more functional manner – came later.

So in beholding creation, Adam and Eve were moved by the Spirit to sing?

You can say that.

Well, that seems to make sense. But what about your own songs? What do you consider your best piece of writing?

Two works are especially liked by the critics – *Circus of the Sun* and *21 Pages*. And people enjoy *Sea and Sky*, *Psalms*, *Dialogues*, and *Mogador's Book*.

Circus of the Sun is an early work, and is lyrical. Afterwards, you primarily wrote in a minimalist-abstract style. Did you ever go back to the lyrical mode?

No, I don't believe that I ever again wrote in a style closely comparable to what is in *Circus of the Sun*. But I was in a special place, then, with the Cristiani Circus. It was, you might say, a lyrical experience.

Sharing the Flame

Some poems are sonic creations, meant to be read aloud. Are yours?

Actually, that's the best way to do them and get them. Even if you are alone in a room, the best thing you can do is read aloud. And if you are moved to at all, you might make up your own tune to go along with the verse. Try singing the poems. In fact, these kinds of things are very good to do with many different types of writing. I'm sure you remember when we went through the Ten Commandments the other day, reading them aloud, you remarked how your understanding of them was heightened.

Yes, I did feel closer to the text. And from what you've been saying, it seems that you strongly encourage reader participation. Although you are primarily writing for yourself, your few words give the reader the space to ponder and reflect aloud – the words may be readily voiced.

Good, good. That's right. I like to think that they evoke too. The words call forth, they awaken...

When you are alone up here, do you read your poems out loud to yourself?

I do. You really hear all of yourself participating in the process of understanding. It also helps in the memorization of the verse too. I think Homer and the early poets knew what they were doing – reading aloud is good for the soul. It puts everything out in the open.

Do you believe that the pronounced word changes the environment? In Genesis, God speaks, and reactions in the environment take place. In a much lesser sense, can humans do the same?

Well, once again, I really do think that it is the perceived meaning of the word that has the ability to create new situations. In this sense, the word, once understood, is communicating. The pronunciation of the word isn't the main thing, except in making the word easier to understand. Now I'm not ruling out any subliminal effect a spoken word may have, but as to the pronounced word having a mystical consequence, that's out of my range. I mean, that sounds like one of those advanced courses, son. (Laughter). See, for me, it's all about communication. By definition, this is an attempt to unite two people by getting a message from one to another. And there are related words such as commune, community, and communion. However, the important thing is to communicate in a gentle way, without forcing the words.

I'm remembering now a line from one of your journals: "Don't try to say something convincing; try to say something true."

That's right. Communication simply *is* – there's no reason to force anything. It's authentic. There's no need for persuasion. When somebody starts to persuade, inflection and projection may twist meaning. That kind of thing makes me narrow my eyes a bit. I prefer to communicate rather than persuade. I think it is enough to say, "He who has ears let him hear." But if you are a talented persuader, if that's your gift, pray heaven you'll be persuading people to do the right thing.

You have said that the "right thing" is easier to do if you know yourself. Yet in your book Dialogues *you ask, "What do you love – me, or Jesus in me?" And the response is "Jesus in me." What about the "me"?*

Well, I think I can answer you this way: I love you, and what I love about you is your inner and eternal fire which we all reveal and share, each of us in a unique way.

In appreciating and celebrating the divine core within each of us, do you feel yourself to be a "witness poet"? Just like St. John the Baptist points to Jesus, do you ultimately point to God through your verse?

There's no other place I'd want to point to, my boy.

That must be why your writing imparts a barren, "ascetic style." In fact, your sparsely structured poems resemble mantras. Like mantras, they tend to have a simple, cyclic, repetitive quality. Comparisons may be made with the famous "Jesus Prayer."[11]

That's certainly possible. I like the Jesus Prayer. Good prayers oftentimes read like poems.

Do you think that in a singular way, your concentrated, mantra-like verse is helping to slow down your readers and also the feverish pace of society?

If my writing helps to slow things down, that's wonderful. And we've got to slow down! As we are constantly increasing our speed, we are simultaneously losing our space. We have so much power, but where do we go with it?

That sounds like what happens on the Golden Gate Bridge during rush hour!

(Laughter). Now that's something to reflect on. But I can't say it enough: *Think slow, move slow.*

Yes, as the Taoists intone, "Only to the mind that is still does the whole universe surrender."

Sure, because it's only when we slow down, relax, that we can really understand anything. When we're calm and living in a state of non-coercion, things sink comfortably in. Living, listening, learning, and loving become so much easier.

Can your poems then be seen as creative meditations because of their calming, centring nature?

They could be, yes. In fact, whatever is done gently, mindfully, soul-centredly helps us to focus on what's important.

And what's important?

Whatever your heart wants to say.

Hearing Oneself Think

Robert, can you explain how your lifelong interest in kabbalistic wisdom[12] relates to your writing?

I started to study the Kabbalah as a young man, when I was visiting the library of the Jewish Theological Seminary in New York. For me it was a way of learning how to be more receptive to divine influence. The Hebrew word *kabbalah* has to do with receiving, how to better receive and perceive holy wisdom in the world. It's a way of love and revelation, how to serve God and help out creation. Kabbalistic lore is filled with so many marvellous

Lax with visiting artists and writers. From left to right: Galatea Psonis of New York, Markus Rötzer of Vienna, Ulf T. Knaus of Salzburg, Gianvito Lo Greco of Rome, Robert Lax, and Steve Georgiou of San Francisco (in front).

S.T. Georgiou, Robert Lax and Gianvito Lo Greco at the waterfront in Skala.

"Spirit Lessons by the Sea." Lax and the author experiment with shadows.

"Let your glances flash together like water in sunlight." Exchanging greetings in Skala.

Lax with visiting fishermen from Kalymnos – old friends going back more than thirty years.

Lax inside the Arion café in Skala.

"It'll be a solo ascent this time." The sage returns
home in the late evening.

"There's a big white bird wheeling over the waves." Captain Robo (Robert Lax) looks out the window of his hermitage.

anecdotes... I paid particular attention to the thirteenth-century kabbalist Abraham Abulafia, who focused on the mystical contemplation of letters. He emphasized meditating on the pure forms of letters and on the holy name of the Most High, so that consciousness comes to expand. It's interesting how the arts critic Richard Kostelanetz recognized him as an early concrete poet, and I think I may have encountered him in that way too. Abulafia's descriptions about how to prepare for holy contemplation and writing are also good to read – very much based on formality and ritual and the idea that every letter is sacred.

Do you approach your writing the same way?

Sometimes I do contemplate or centre myself before writing, but as far as any elaborate ritual goes, no.

Yet you are a man of ritual. I see how precisely you fold things, how you carefully place things around your house...

(Laughter). Well, if I'm doing that, it's only to help me remember where I put things and what it is I have to do!

But isn't that what ritual partly does? Through practice, psychosomatic rhythms are created which you can meld and move with. Aren't ritual and memory interconnected?

Sure, you can say that. In this way, ritual helps to keep one flowing, focused, awake.

You know, the Buddha made the statement "I am awake," and you oftentimes state, "I write to hear myself think." Is there a link here?

Well, I do believe there's something related there. Writing has so much to do with listening to yourself, with being awake to the present moment. And I can much more identify with the word "awake" than, say, the word "alert," because "alert" seems to hint at impending burnout. It's not flowing — it's too immediate.

Do you think that the high-tech world we live in has contributed to that frantic sense of immediacy? Is the computer to blame for the stressful times we live in?

Perhaps there's something there. However, the computer is also a very useful instrument, and can save one time. Like anything else, it must be used wisely.

You know, a few years ago, I was surprised to see an old Macintosh Classic in your back room. Has the computer helped you to amplify your creativity?

Although I always like new challenges, I really had no intention of getting a computer. A friend gave it to me. But since I've had it, I'm not exactly sure how it has affected my writing. I've done some work at the computer and it doesn't seem to be much different from the typewriter I used to use. The typewriter sure was noisier, and in making spelling corrections, the computer has certainly become more advantageous. Overall, I'd say it has helped me in being more ordered. There's a particular neatness to the device.

Do you find it difficult to compose on the computer? Does the pencil and notepad have a more organic feel?

Well, an interesting thing about the computer is that it is electric just like our bodies are electric, just like our thoughts are electric, all composed of wavelengths... No, I don't think it's hard creating with the computer. Part of the reason has to do with how I got the machine. Since it was given to me by a friend, I think of it as a new friend in the house. It's even entered my dreams. I have dreamed of myself working at the computer, and they are good dreams.

Do you think society may get too computerized?

It's all a question of balance. After you sit for a while, you have to get up; after you stand for too long, you have to sit down. Anything can get out of balance. Like our old friend Aristotle said, "Moderation in all things." But you know and I know that the computer is here to stay. I mean, the computer – something that can pick up messages and process information, just like a net catching fish – is knit up into the very framework of the cosmos.

Are you possibly saying that the Internet has divine implications?

There is the Creator, and from the Creator extends creative evolution. I don't think it's by accident that fishing nets sort of resemble computer circuitry, and cities, from the air, look like computer chips. There is a message system already in place in the cosmos, and maybe we're intuitively

147

and creatively building upon that. We're good at clueing in.

I think it was Marshall McLuhan who said, "Through electronics we have extended the human nervous system into outer space."

That's very good. I like that.

Working the Dream Field

What advice can you give young writers?

Well, I'll say the same thing I've said to you, Gary,[13] Mike,[14] John,[15] Galatea,[16] and other writers I've known over the years. Studying the dictionary from time to time can't hurt – inside are the seeds you're going to plant in your field. And you can't go wrong reading as much as you can, reviewing different styles and seeing how word placement has an effect on meaning and inspirational flow. Two verse forms which I think are excellent exercises for the poet are the Haiku and Sonnet. It's good to have classic forms through which to channel and exercise the flow of expression. And to all writers I say go out and get a big notebook, a good comfortable pen, and just dive in and write. *Write, write, write!* Don't think about judging your work – just spill it out, and you'll discover that it's a self-refining process. So keep on writing. Do that for as long as you can manage to, whether it's three weeks, three months, or whatever. Don't even glance through it until one of those long stretches has passed. Write what you have to write, put it away, and don't worry about it – it'll be playing its music to you in your dreams and waking moments. As long as you stick to a rhythm, you'll find themes that keep recurring because they are the ones that are most a part of you. With time, you'll be able to determine the ups and downs of your own creative cycle and tap into the themes that are closest to your heart. Keeping a dream journal may help with this. Oh, and one more thing – don't be concerned with what other writers think of your work. If you are, you're wasting energy and time, unless, of course, your critics are giving you helpful hints. The bottom line is to believe in your original vision, your unique voice. Write to keep your vision going, and everything else will follow.

What about creative writing and healing? Is writing, particularly poetry, a restorative process? The Greek word "poet" means creator. So aren't poets life-givers, even "rejuvenators," since they contribute new life to the universe?

Just by being here we are contributing new life to the universe! And as far as creativity and health go, sure there's restorative potential there because self-discovery is involved. This is therapeutic. What is therapeutic in me might also be in you. We are interrelated. So people might like somebody's writing because they feel a sense of communal spiritual benefit. And when these connections are perceived, what ultimately happens is that people *relax* – they see how life is a shared journey.

Every so often you tell me how the prerequisite for good writing is relaxation. How so?

A state of calmness is not only important for good writing but for good living too. It's preparatory to work. If you're uptight, you can't work well, think well, or pray well. When you're relaxed, you can listen more, hear all the voices, dream more too. That way you make the right choices and can form a better plan for living. I just wrote a poem which may illustrate this.

I'd like to hear it.

"What should I do?" asked the wind.
And the voice said, "Blow, blow, blow."
"What should I do?" asked the river.
And the voice said, "Flow, flow, flow."

Again, we go with the flow. It sounds so simple, almost childlike.

(Laughter). Well, I guess it becomes so.

You know, a while back a priest told me, "What greater joy can there be than to be called a child of God?"

That's beautiful, Steve.

But how do we begin to become "children of God"?

By becoming what we already are. We are all God's children and we have always been loved by Him. You realize that more when you get relaxed.

How?

Aside from all the meditational techniques and the necessity for quiet space, making lists is a good way to begin to relax. This might sound too ordinary, but lists take things out of your mind, they help to unclutter it. You can always refer to lists later, so that what's in your mind is always new, welcoming the moment. When I was somewhere in my thirties, I made two lists – on one was what I wanted in life, and on the other I listed why I wasn't getting it. Both lists eventually helped me to figure out what I really needed, what was essential.

And what was that?

Simply the grace and peace of heaven. Anything more just seemed to get in the way.

Well, that's certainly getting down to basics!

You bet.

Soul Scribe

Robert, in our past walks and talks together, you've mentioned that good writing can bring peace to the world.

Yes, that's true – inevitably it does. But it's not enough to just write peaceful things and then go off and live in an uncompassionate manner. You have to live what you are writing, and if you are writing from your heart, if you are a "soul-scribe," good things will happen. This reminds me of a religious meeting I went to in New York. Everybody was talking on and on about the love and the peace and the sweetness of Jesus. Then somebody stood up and said, "It's time we stopped talking about Jesus and started acting more like Him!"

And how do we go about doing that?

Gently, kindly. No flag waving. I mean, you shouldn't try too hard to do a good thing – you don't scream and shout compassion! It's better if you relax and do whatever good you can in a calm, loving, steady manner. Do one thing at a time, each thing as best you can, even if it's as simple as writing your name. Just keep at it – be like dripping spring water. Water, simply by falling over and over on the same stone, eventually shapes it. You see, the good you will be doing will catch on, simply through example. And as long as you do your part, you'll be helping others to do theirs. Over the years I've found that if you do the right thing, somehow the rest of the world gets "righted" to. There's a Zen saying: "When a single flower blooms, it's Spring everywhere."

Somehow it always seems to go back to how all things are interrelated, interdependent.

That's because they are! Look at nature. I've heard it said that when a little drop of rain carries a bit of dirt off the shore and into the sea, there are repercussions that extend from deep within the earth to the farthest reaches of the galaxy. So who knows what one loving act can do? Who can trace the measure of a single peaceful word said from the heart?

That's all so true. Your words help to convince me how poets and writers can be natural peacemakers.

Well, I think that peace has to do with resolving problems in a non-violent way. As Gandhi would say, weapons rebound. I believe that a poet, no matter what his or her theme is, tries to work in an ultimately harmonious, integrative manner. Inclusiveness appeals to me. Why else do so many stars shine in one sky? Honestly, I can't think of any poets I respect that are writing hurtful tirades, polemical things that wound and divide. All the poets that I have come to admire communicate and enlighten in understandable and liberating ways. And I think peace works that way too. I think the astute poet can give a foretaste of what real peace might be like. Poets demonstrate that communion between people does not have to be an exchange of growls, as history has conditioned us to think. Instead, poets can show how we can sing together, laugh together. All the arts can encourage unity. We are meant to network. Everything exists to form relationships. United, things flow.

What if people just don't like each other?

They should listen to the poets and the artists and the movie makers and the priests and try to sing and create themselves. The cosmos is a big canvas. I think everybody should get out their pens and prayers and cameras and composition books and paints and brushes! There's room for everybody. I mean, get out the dancing shoes!

That's great! So how would you feel if you were defined as a major spiritual poet of the twentieth century?

(Laughter). Oh, for heaven's sake, that would be absolute nonsense, that's all!

Is something wrong with the title? Don't you consider yourself to be spiritually gifted — a creative mystic?

Well, I'm very happy if someone simply considers me to be a poet.

Wow! You really are a blue jeans kind of guy—stone ground, rough cut!

And you better believe it! Whammo!

Bam! Wham! Kaboom!

Zoom! Zoom! Varoooom!

Slam! Wham! Zowie!

Zow! Pow! Tao!

(Laughter). OK, I think it's time for both of us to go out for a walk. But before we do, let me ask you this. In the days when you were following the travelling circus, you had a close friend named Mogador,

an acrobat and member of the Cristiani family. You titled a long poem to him called Mogador's Book. *Why was he special to you?*

He was a genuine companion. He was an admirable, articulate, exemplary person, a good and true friend. We got along well, partly because he knew English better than anyone in his family. He had developed a taste for poetical metaphysics and was reading reflective things like *The Prophet* by Kahlil Gibran. His character was upright, quietly noble, truly a remarkable man. He still drops me a line from time to time.

In speaking of Mogador, I thought you might like to close by reading part of a letter that you had written to your circus friend a long time ago, a letter which appears at the end of Mogador's Book.

Why, I'd be happy to, and I think Mogador would be too.

Mogador, I still haven't gotten to say the thing I want to say about you and the whole family. It is that, to a greater degree than almost anyone I know, you are what you are. You are an acrobat in a family of acrobats. And you have arrived at that generation in the family which is most to be desired, the time of ripeness, the moment of fullest awareness of function and responsibility of producing beauty, songs of praise...

Think, Mogador, of the freedom in a world of bondage, a world expelled from Eden; the freedom of the priest, the artist, and the acrobat. In a world of men condemned to earn their bread by the sweat of their brows, the liberty of those, who, like the lilies of the field, live by playing. For playing is like Wisdom before the face of the Lord. Their play is praise. Their praise is prayer. This play, like the ritual gestures of the priest, is characterized by grace; heavenly grace unfolding, flowering and reflected in the physical grace of the player.

I had a friend, a Hindu monk named Brahmachari,[11] whose monastery near Calcutta was called Sri Agnan, which he translated as "The Playground of the Lord." That is the key to the whole matter, the monks playing joyously and decorously before the Lord, praising the Lord. The playground, though sown with tares, is a reflection of Eden. I think there can be a "Circus of the Lord."

For we are all wanderers in the earth, and pilgrims. We have no permanent habitat here. The migration of people for foraging and exploiting can become, with grace (in the latter days), a travelling circus. Our tabernacle must in its nature be a temporary tabernacle.

We are wanderers in the earth, but only a few of us in each generation have discovered the life of charity, the living from day to day, receiving our gifts gratefully through grace, and rendering them, multiplied through grace, to the Giver. That is the meaning of your expansive, outward arching gesture of the arm in the landing, the grateful rendering, the gratitude and giving.[18]

---

¹ See *33 Poems* by Robert Lax, p. 70. Edited by Thomas Kellein. New York: New Directions, 1988.

² Moschos Lagouvardos, a native Greek, was an early admirer and devotee of Lax, having first met him on Kalymnos in the late 1960s. Like many people who have encountered Lax, Lagouvardos was impressed with the poet's quiet way of life, and felt a deep and abiding peace in his presence. His memories of Lax may be read in the first chapter of his book, *One Quiet Man,* Athens, 2000 (in Greek). Lagouvardos writes of how Lax had the particular ability to share silence. He and Lax would spend long hours together saying nothing yet understanding everything. For Lagouvardos, the quiet time spent with Lax was "serene, indescribably sweet."

³ Philotheus Boehner (1901–1955) was the eminent German medievalist and polymath who was appointed the first director of the Franciscan Institute at St. Bonaventure University. Under his influence the university became internationally known as a centre for the study of William Ockham, a pivotal fourteenth century Franciscan theologian. Boehner, equally versatile in theology and the sciences,(he held a doctorate in biology), was a mentor and friend to both Lax and Merton. He was well known for his kindness and the spiritual direction he gave to many students.

⁴ Emil Antonucci, illustrator, film maker, publisher, and current arts editor at *Commonweal* magazine, was an early admirer and publisher of Lax's work. Other early publishers of Lax's poetry include Maurizio Nannucci of Florence, Michael Lastnite of Vermont, and Bernhard Moosbrugger of Zurich.

⁵ The artist Robert Kagnowski was an early friend and admirer of Lax. One of his paintings, resembling an oriental abstract, was usually on display in Lax's hermitage.

⁶ See Merton's *The Way of Chuang Tzu,* 1965.

⁷ See *The ABC's of Robert Lax,* 183.

8 Denise Levertov, American poet. Levertov particularly appreciated Lax's *Circus of the Sun,* which she compared with St. Francis of Assisi's *Canticle of the Sun,* See *The ABC's of Robert Lax,* 181.

9 In the summers of 1939 and 1940, Lax, Merton, and others led a bohemian lifestyle at the cottage of Benjamin Marcus, husband to Lax's older sister, Gladys. Interestingly, Gladys (Gladio, as Lax sometimes called her) had a dream during the late 1930s in which she saw people from all over the world coming to visit the cottage ("Robert Lax—Coming Home," by Jack Kelly. *The Merton Seasonal.* Lax Memorial Issue. Spring 2001).

10 *A Catch of Anti-letters* (Sheed & Ward, 1978) is a collection of zany, fascinating letters exchanged between Lax and Merton that Merton edited prior to his accidental death in Thailand. Herein, Lax and Merton may be found addressing one another in a bizarre, unconventional manner. Lax had been known to sometimes echo this good natured "eccentric exuberance" in everyday conversation with close friends. At the same time, "electric expressions" such as *Pow* and *Zowie* may also be interpreted in a Zen manner, as they are meant to awaken people to the power of the present moment. Perhaps most importantly, however, these exclamations do have specific definitions. In a letter to the author (2.17.1995) Lax wrote: "*Pow* is for Power. *Wham* is for Wisdom and *Zowie* is for Love."

11 The "Jesus Prayer" is an early Christian (Hesychast) prayer which reads, "Jesus Christ, Son of God, Have Mercy Upon Me, A Sinner" (sometimes "A Sinner" is omitted). The reciter of the prayer is encouraged to repeat and internalize the phrase until it proceeds spontaneously from the heart. For more on the prayer, see *The Jesus Prayer.* Archimandrite Lev Gillet. New York: St. Vladimir's Seminary Press, 1987. Interestingly, Hesychast thought and practice bears similarities with yoga, which Lax also integrated into his life. For the relationship between Hesychasm and yoga, see *Yoga and the Jesus Prayer Tradition* by Thomas Matus, Mahwah, NJ: Paulist Press, 1984.

12 "Kabbalah" means *receiving,* in other words, receiving the divine wisdom which is constantly manifesting itself in the cosmos. The *Zohar*

is the canonical text of the Kabbalah, and was composed in 1280 by the Spanish Jewish mystic Moses de Leon, who in turn drew upon earlier biblical and rabbinic literature. The Kabbalah influenced many Hebrew communities and movements through the centuries, especially Hasidism, the eighteenth-century revivalist movement in Eastern Europe. The great aim of the kabbalist is to discover the hidden light of God shining in the world; in the process, a greater sense of harmony is cultivated and transmitted throughout creation.

[13] Gary Bauer, American writer and a friend of Lax for many years, has intermittently lived on Patmos since 1976.

[14] Michael McGregor is an essayist and fiction writer. His articles on Lax include "Turning the Jungle into a Garden: A Visit with Robert Lax" (*Poets and Writers Magazine,* March–April 1997) and "After the Circus Goes By," *The Merton Seasonal.* Robert Lax Memorial Issue, Spring 2001.

[15] John Lavitt, a longtime friend of Lax, is a poet and screenwriter residing in Los Angeles.

[16] Galatea Psonis is a New York writer, singer, and dancer who regularly visits and performs in Greece.

[17] For more on Brahmachari, see *"Origins,"* the first dialogue section of this book.

[18] Robert Lax. *Mogador's Book.* Edited by P.J. Spaeth. Zurich: Pendo-Verlag. 1992, 66–70.

ART

The juggler
is playing,
throwing and catching,
resting,
returning;
practicing
his art.
He is here,
is there,
moving swiftly:
one who hides
from cloud
to spring
to mountain cleft,
to a voice
within a flame.

Robert Lax,
from *Circus of the Sun*

Robert Lax's minimalist and visually-oriented writing has been strongly identified with the painting of the abstract expressionist Ad Reinhardt, a close friend of Lax and a member of the "inner circle" at Columbia. Just as one might focus upon a "Black Painting" by Reinhardt and eventually glimpse a subtly painted cross pattern take shape within the exceedingly dark canvas, so one might study Lax's poetry at length and discover new meanings, as seen in the following "colour poem" by Lax, excerpted from *The Light, The Shade*, 1989.

black
black

white
white

red
red

blue
blue

Though at first glance the poem may appear overwhelmingly simple, if not elementary, this observation would have delighted Lax, who understood that the same "free and natural simplicity" applies to everything in the cosmos and most primarily to God Himself. True and authentic things, be they colours or living entities, simply *are* – their pure presence does not require a detailed, convoluted explanation. Too much of human "doing" oftentimes obscures the pure and divine reality of simple "being." Thus while the poem may challenge some readers, its unaffected and familiar beauty is open to all.

The colours expressed in "Black-White-Red-Blue" suggest an infinite range of images, all of which are equally valid, since everyone brings their own unique life experiences to the poem. But certainly some general observations may be made. To begin, the refreshingly open arrangement of the poem allows it to be read from top to bottom or bottom to top, consequently the eye takes any direction it pleases. At the same time, the precise, clean arrangement of the couplets not only indicates a devotion to purity and clarity, but may also bring to mind a "frame by frame cinema sequence," as Lax himself suggested.[1] Life is therefore a colourful movie in which all things, including tones and shades, play vital and irreplaceable parts. Each colour is to be savoured, to be read slowly, mindfully, reverently so that it might speak according to its nature.

Ultimately, the poem is not an end in itself, but is an utterly simple yet carefully designed creation leading to a higher reality – the words form an iconic portal through which the imaginative spirit might pass and make contact with the Creator. In proceeding from the bottom of the poem and reading upward, we depart from the blue of the sea and sky and rise toward the blazing red fire of heaven. We then soar through the white purity of God and then at last plunge into His black infinity and unknowable Being. Read in this upward linear fashion, the poem may reflect the transitive ascension of the soul. And if the verse is read from top to bottom, one may visualize a brilliant and divine ray of light descending from heaven to earth (changing as it filters through the levels of creation), or may see the black night giving way to a white dawn. A fiery noon follows, leading to a crimson sunset which fades into an intense blue darkness.

How the space is arranged in the poem is also important. It not only aids in the transition between colours but points to the "invisible divine Nature," to the heavenly Void "pregnant with possibility," to the unseen, dream-like realm of the Spirit out of which words and colours are born and into which they shall inevitably return. Therefore Lax arranges the "empty" space on his page as might a painter addressing his canvas so that a "Light beyond light" might steadily shine through. His work is not an end in itself, but points to a Presence in which the whole of life shares and participates.

Building Bridges

What do you think is the function and purpose of art?

Art has to do with the transformation of consciousness. And I see art as a harmonic enterprise because it has the capability to make the world a better place. As you know, I particularly appreciate the search for peace through art. The artist who is peace-loving seeks not to direct attention to himself and is not interested in becoming a guru-like figure – he simply creates from the heart, doing the best he can as he gives expression to his soul. In the process, both darkness and light are unveiled and explored. Essentially, the artist feels for balance. Ultimately, this intuitive quest can offer something valuable to the world.

Recently an increasing number of books have been published on the healing attributes of art. How does art heal?

Well, if you were to meditate upon an aesthetic creation and experience a good feeling, I think that would make you happier and somehow healthier. And I think one of the reasons why people go to museums is because they can identify with the soul-shaping voices they hear in the art, voices the viewers themselves might not be able to readily express. But I really do feel that art especially heals the artist – it is the making of art in itself which aids in self-discovery and inner catharsis. I mean, at its core, creating art teaches one how to become a better person, because when all is said and done, the dedicated artist is really crafting himself. And I'm sure you've heard how a patient who can't express himself to his doctor is in a far worse way than one who can. So what you can do through art is bring out your dreams, fears, aspirations, anxieties, even if your creation is a momentary sketch or squiggle. This process relaxes the soul which, as you know, is a good thing – tranquility is the basis in attempting to know oneself.

How long have you held these views?

From an early time I felt this way. When I was editor of *PAX* magazine,[2] a publication devoted to fostering peace through the arts, that's what we were centred on. My friends and I believed that artists could work for communal harmony and well-being simply by being good artists in their own particular ways. My old friend Ad Reinhardt held the same views. We all believed that artists could work for peace primarily by being true to their craft, by really centring themselves and working their gifts.

So centred work produces good vibes?

Yes, but not because you're thinking about the vibes. The good vibes happen because you're thinking about your work.

I see. What makes for a good, productive artist?

Someone who listens deeply to themselves and then gives shape to the genuine stirrings of the heart. And since people are doing this all over the world, an "international language of the soul" may be said to exist. This language crosses all barriers and is a form of communication which people from very diverse backgrounds can understand and employ. Just as scientists and others have established international forms of expression, I feel that artists from all over the world should increasingly get in touch with each other and joyfully share their dreams and visions. Already this is happening, and I feel that new dimensions of the heart will be unveiled in this way. Art is a wonderful bridgemaker. The whole thing is about helping us to find out who we are.

I know that you like photographic art, and you have taken many fine photographs yourself, especially focusing on fishermen, landscapes, shadows, and silhouettes. Why do you find photography so appealing?

Photography is complementary to my writing because both are about looking – learning how to look, how to see. With a good still black-and-white image, the writer can do a lot. Over the years, I've gone back to numerous photos that I've taken and they have helped me in my work. In writing my journals, I've made references to photos I have taken in the past. I study the images carefully and can always discover new details, resonances, lights and shadows. Good photos point to an inner something that can be shared, just like poems and dreams do.

Once you told me that many of your photos were lost in a fire. How did that happen?

The fire's origin remains unknown. It started in Michael Lastnite's house over in Vermont. At the time he was publishing my poems in booklet form. As I recall, my negatives were spread out on a table when the fire started.

He managed to save a few, but by the time he got to the blaze, hundreds went up in smoke. And even those that were saved got lost in transit to the National Library.

What a loss!

Yes, it was hard to get over.

Now what about movies? Since earlier you had made short films with Emil Antonucci in New York, did you shoot any films out here?

No, but I think I've told you how over the years others have come over here and filmed me reading my work and that sort of thing. Recently, Cine Nomad,[3] based in Munich, made a creative documentary about me titled *Why Should I Buy A Bed When All That I Want Is Sleep? Three Windows* has also been recently released. This movie is a three-screen installation film that is visiting Munich, Berlin, Zurich, and Tokyo.

As you know, artists have come over to Patmos hoping to meet you. If you could speak to them now, what would you say?

Well, I'd tell them the same thing I told my artist friends back in high school – *do what you want!* In those days, when I was the Editor of the *New Town Lantern*, the school paper, I told every artist I knew then to create whatever art they felt brimming inside them. Go right ahead, I said, get to work, and don't let anybody or anything get in your way, particularly the critics. So a lot of artistic contributions came into the magazine, some really nice ones, some really strange ones. And I was much more inclined to run the atypical contributions and encourage their creators to do new things. It then came to me how that would be one of the things I would want to do all of my life – to encourage and promote art, to see what new and wonderful things might be done! I wanted to give everyone the spark to create because I understood the blessings of self-discovery and free expression. Art opens our eyes. We see the world differently, lovingly, with the uninhibited joy of children. Art helps us to be happy, and in the moment.

I really do think that art is important to you because it is a vehicle through which everything you value is accomplished. Attention to the moment, self-discovery, communion with others, reconnection with the divine, a going with the flow, a kind of mystical travelling, a kind of dreaming…it's all there.

You're right. The value of art as divine expression and creative evolution cannot be overestimated. Art is certainly about dreaming, about being intuitively connected with that creative dream, that freedom-vision…

God is an artist too.

The Master.

And when artists work, they are called upon to continue the creative flow.

You can say that. Creating helps us to flow with the Creator, and with His love. As co-creators, we were meant to be tenders of the garden and sustainers of creation.

And how do we nurture and sustain?

Through unconditional love. That's the bottom line, son. Everything is here because of love. That's why we were created – to love, and creation was set up to make love possible. Love keeps things going, not just for now, but for forever. Love gives life and makes sure what's around today will be around tomorrow. Love sets us out on the journey and ensures our safe return. It's about compassion, it's what the cosmos best responds to…

So when people do compassionate acts, do you believe that a loving energy born of their acts radiates out to help others?

You know I do! It's sort of like dropping a stone into a pond – the ripples affect the entire body of water. And they spread, emanate, awakening responses in the heart.

In the same way that goodness radiates from good acts, do you feel that mystical vibrations and emanations issue out of a painting? There are some who believe that a type of "spirit resonance" may exude out of a work of art.

Well, that's good to hear, and it makes for a wonderful round of discussion at the local arts café, but my feeling about painting, especially with regard to Reinhardt and other abstract artists, is that a painting does not work as an "emanating creation" but more like a magnet. The artist draws you toward the painting, and you are pulled in. A doorway of sorts is created, and through it you enter. Sculpture, I think, can do the same thing. So I believe that you are drawn into the artwork, and once you have crossed over, you start noticing interesting things in the creation. I remember Reinhardt's series of "Black Paintings." If you were to look at one, all you might immediately see is a large black painting, but as you look into it, a cross begins to appear out of the darkness, and, after looking at the cross for a while, it fades back into the original blackness. At least, that's what some viewers have experienced.

Yes, I've seen one over at Berkeley, in the University of California Art Museum. It's powerful watching that cross-like design slowly materialize out of the apophatic darkness. And I believe that Reinhardt gifted one of these earlier "Black Paintings" to Merton. He felt that it would aid in Merton's meditation.

That's right, and I'm glad you have one over there. Reinhardt always felt that art teaches people how to see and wake up to what *is*. He really believed that artworks may serve as objects of contemplation.

So we delve into the inner dimensions of a painting and see new, revelatory things. Then the time comes when we walk away. What are we taking with us?

Well, you just said it — *we take something with us*. The viewing experience is like diving into the sea. You may find a pearl, and, if you do, well, come up with it, and share it with others. I think art is like a dose of salts. It wakes you up, starts a process in you that can take any manner of metamorphosis. You see, art has an infinite range of effect on people, but, in the end, I'm sure it works toward some universal, all-embracing synthesis. What's important to keep in mind is that the artwork is not an end in itself, but acts as a catalyst to spiritual discovery. It has to do with a greater process partly brought on by the artist who keeps the vision alive.

What about the place of enlightenment in creating art? Do you think that the artist should work only after experiencing some sort of illumination?

Some people get new insights before creation, some during, some after, and some artists experience all three in a sequential process. There's nothing really definitive in making art, otherwise that might restrict the very meaning of art. We're dealing with creative freedom here, and that includes all forms of expression, be it painting, sculpting, writing, singing, dancing...I think that if illumination were a prerequisite to creation, we'd have very few artists. But, of course, the joy of enlightenment may indeed catalyze artistic expression and oftentimes does.

Art as Art

Who are some of the great twentieth-century artists you have admired?

Mondrian, de Chirico, Cézanne, Matisse, Picasso, Klee, Reinhardt...there are many others. I remember Brancusi's "Bird in Space" really got me thinking about the power of abstract art.

Has abstract art reached its limits? Is it time to go back to figure drawing and landscape scenes?

Well, those things are generally cyclical. The pendulum swings back and forth, like anything else. Now I may be well off on this but I've been thinking that abstract art is a summing up of what's been going on in art since art began – a conscious pooling together of styles which synthesize into a timeless and essential field of line and colour, of spirit, rhythm, and thought. And if that's the case, abstract art will always be in vogue.

Some of your abstract poems, like "Black and White Oratio," remind me of Ad Reinhardt's paintings, especially his "Black Series." Is there any relationship here?

I picked up a number of my ideas about abstraction, colour, and things like that from Reinhardt. We always talked about art and its influences and when it came time to create, we were both ready to work, each in our own way. Yet we both were intent on reducing things down to the barest minimum. So we abstracted down to essentials in order to show things in their purest form, as they really are.

So would you say that when a viewer sees a painting by Reinhardt or reads one of your minimalist poems, he or she receives the subject in its purest form?

I would hope so. Purity, stillness, timelessness… but it's up to the viewer-reader to search for any and all meanings. In both art and life, one begins where one is, the only place where one can really be.

Let's say we have an actual tree. Then I study a painting of an abstracted tree. That abstraction may help me to glimpse the tree in its purest form?

It may.

So in a way, it's like a circle. There is an original tree which I see. Then I view the abstracted essence of the tree, gazing upon its pure, rarefied form. Then I see the original tree again, but with new eyes.

Yes, that's good.

That sounds quite a bit like a statement made by D.T. Suzuki:[4] "When we begin Zen, mountains are mountains, but, after a while, they are no longer mountains; then, eventually, they are mountains once more, but with a difference."

Good. Yes, I'm familiar with that, and I really like it.

Tell me, when Reinhardt came back from his numerous trips to Asia, did he talk to you about his feelings on Eastern art? What did he think about Eastern art in relationship to Western art?

We often talked about his Asian treks and discoveries and I do believe he found wonderful things out there that impressed him, considerably more than what he had found in the West. I remember how he used to tell me that while you get the dome and the towering linear spire in the West, in the East you get the full circle. I'm pretty sure he liked the full circle. A circle nicely unifies end point and origin.

What do you think of Reinhardt's "negation of religion"? Did Reinhardt feel that religion can be idolatrous and impede spiritual perception and growth?

I think Reinhardt felt that even religious systems can calcify the Spirit if maximum attention is devoted to the system rather than the Spirit which sustains the system. Merton and myself would never think of Reinhardt as being anti-spiritual. He just didn't like the idea of art being used for spiritual propaganda and commercialism. Reinhardt emphasized purity, a purity grounded on the spiritual depth of the artist and on the artist's consistent dedication to the work at hand. Hence his well-known credo, "Art as art." And when he went to the Gethsemani monastery with me to visit Merton, he never lost his sense of the sacred nor his perennial sense of humour. He knew that he had been called to a particular vocation and that was to be an artist, not a formal theologian. He was devout to his vocation – he was a spiritual inspiration to me. He really tried to be the best artist he could be.

You and Reinhardt were great friends going back to high school. Did you keep in touch with him through the years?

Yes, we sent letters and postcards to each other.

Were your letters as off the wall[5] as the ones you sent to Merton?

They had a zip of their own. Reinhardt's postcards always had funny squiggles and strange maps and arcane messages, all done in his careful hand.

In addition to Reinhardt, what other artists were friends of yours?

Reinhardt was closest to me, but there were others, friends like Willem de Kooning, Robert Motherwell, and Roberto Matta. All three of them were good friends. Who else? Well, those three stand out at the moment.

What was the New York Artist's Club like?

It was a good place. Reinhardt brought me with him to the meetings. There were mostly painters and sculptors there. It was down on Cedar Street. The meetings may have been once every few weeks, but I can't recall.

Is that where you met most of your art friends?

I met many of them down there through Reinhardt. Others I had already met at Columbia, again through Reinhardt. I met very few on my own. As for Matta, I met him in Paris. Once, when I was low on cash, he let me live in his studio for a while.

What were the meetings like at the Club?

They were lively. They had animated discussions, and somebody would chair the talks to keep them from getting too far out of hand. But there was no real rough stuff.

Once in a while de Kooning may have gotten into more of a fighting mode, but he was a good boy.

Live and Help Live

What do you — hey, it looks like you've got a big fly in the house!

Well, you know what to do.

Yeah, you've given me lots of experience in fly saving. I guess I'll get the plastic cup in the kitchen?

No, use the one over there by the window.

You know, this is actually a good time to ask you a related question — why do you go to extremes to save any creature, even spiders and cockroaches? You're very careful when you walk down the road so that you won't step on anything moving. And when ants come into your house, you redirect them out of your dwelling with a sugar cube.

Well, you know me — I'd rather cultivate life than destroy it. St. Francis and the Buddha would agree. All creatures are my friends, and all creatures hate pain.

Yes, I would think that even protozoa flee from fire!

So, Uncle Steve, a major rule of life is not to kill anything if you can help it.

But you don't even step on cut flowers you find in the road. Instead, you place them off to the side.

To quote that grace prayer of yours, "Nothing dies." Maybe if we acted like nothing were dead, but rather alive and highly sensitive, we might become more gentle.

(Cupping fly). Like you say, Petros of Patmos, "Gently, gently, slowly, slowly..."

That's right – have you got him? Don't break his leg, now.

Yes, I have him.

Gee, you're getting better at this each time you come over. Now go out to the porch and give him back to the sky. And watch out for the cats!

OK, Robo-Master, liberation stage commencing...

(A minute later). So where did he go?

Wild blue yonder.

Great. Now didn't that make you happy? Isn't that what lasting happiness is about? You had the choice to kill or save, and you saved. You gave life!

You know, Bob, suddenly I'm inspired to say a poem in honour of all creatures. I really am.

Go ahead.

Flys are flying,
Ants are anting,
Cats are catting,
Dogs are dogging.

That's grand, Steve – let me reciprocate:

Bow, Wow,
Meow, Meow,
We go
Wow Wow.

(Laughter). We go Wow Wow?

Yes, that's *us*, California Kid – we behold creation, we nurture it, and we rejoice.

Excellent! Things are simply being what they were created to be.

Ain't it like heaven, Steve?

"All the way to heaven is heaven," like St. Catherine of Siena said.

Blowing in the Wind

What do you think of jazz, Lord Laxmos, King of the Isle of Catmos?

(Laughter). Well, Jive-Man, it's really one of the top art forms. Merton thought so too, and he was a great drummer. Jazz has got all the modulations that are to be found in an expressive, creative language, more so than any of the other arts. But in addition to jazz, I love Bach, and he's got a language all his own.

Hey, I don't know why but right now I'm remembering St. Augustine, how he said that lyrics should always accompany music because the captivating, liberating sound of music was thought to have the power to lead listeners astray.

I can understand why St. Augustine may have felt this way, but I don't agree with his thinking on that point. Music should be allowed to breathe and flow on its own.

Like the Beatles said, "Let it be"?

Yeah, let it all go right on by.

You can't believe how happy I am to hear that, Bobcat.

Well, shucks, I'm just as happy to tell it to you!

(Laughter). Being a lifelong music enthusiast, which musicians have you met over the years?

When I was in New York, I heard classical conductors like Toscanini. And since I was very fond of jazz, I had many friends who were jazz artists. Merton and I went to a lot of clubs. I knew people like Zutty Singleton, Duke Ellington, Johnny Hodges, Jimmy Blanton, Woody Herman. There were so many musicians, artists like Count Basie, Pee Wee Russell, Joe Marsala, Hot Lips Page… much later, I got to know Sun Ra.[6] He was a poet and philosopher as well, just a great guy all around. And I also knew Louis Armstrong, Billie Holiday, and Ella Fitzgerald. Ella even invited me up to her apartment to hear her music there, but I didn't go, couldn't make it. I knew her before she really became famous. She had just come up from the country and was beginning to sing. From the first note she sang, there was no question that she was enormously talented. She was one of those people who used her voice like a musical instrument. She could instantaneously improvise – what a jazz queen.

Now as I recall, you once told me that you knew the young Bob Dylan and went to a number of parties that he also happened to attend.

That's right. In fact, I remember how at one evening party, where artists and musicians were gathering, having cocktails, he and his girl came in. After hanging around for a while, Bob went into a room with his guitar, took some time there, and then came back out and said he'd just written a new song and asked if we'd like to hear it. "Sure," we said. "We like your music. Play it." And the song turned out to be "Blowing in the Wind."

Wow! And you were there when that classic was born. How cool!

And we did like it. We knew his star was rising. He was well on his way.

What a charming, special moment. Talk about being in sync with the flow!

Yes, it was great, it really was good to be there.

Didn't Merton like Dylan a lot?

Sure, he loved him, along with Joan Baez. He would play their songs over and over again. But Dylan really moved him.

So, "Mr. Tambourine Man," did you ever meet the musician and author John Cage?

(Laughter). I heard one of his concerts in New York but did not personally meet him. He's someone who really listens, as in *4 Minutes, 33 Seconds*.

Oh yes, that's the selection where he walks out on stage, sits at the piano, and plays nothing during that time, indicating that the very sounds around us are music.

Yes, and I like that. The music is going on all the time.

Since we're discussing music, can you tell me why you recently wrote to me and advised that I start composing music?

Well, you're obviously a gifted person – I'm not out to embarrass you, but you are, and you're full of energy –

Like everyone else –

Sure, like everyone else. But since my earlier suggestion to you about continuing your writing and theological pursuits and going on to create art turned out to be a very good thing for you, I thought you could go a step further. Music is an even more universal language than painting. It's been said that all the arts point to music. So think about it. We all want Steve to be Steve, and that means *artist* in many ways.

I don't know. Pursuing something like that requires time and dedication.

But I bet you will continue to branch out and do the music venture eventually. Don't worry about going slow.

Just keep at it, 'cause you're the man who can do it. So write those tunes, keep painting those pictures, because it's all part of one big whirling song and dance. Artists can work more than one field. Merton and Rice were both fine drummers.

Did I tell you that I had a dream about Merton some years ago? He was smiling, playing drums in a jazz club, and this was before you told me that he was a drummer and a jazz aficionado. You were in the dream too, but I can't remember what you were doing.

Maybe I was dancing! But isn't that so wonderful – Merton at the drums. And now I remember a dream that I had a while back. I was on a huge canvas and somehow had painted myself into a corner. Then, all at once, I began to hear the music of Duke Ellington, and the music just lifted me right out of the painting. Son, if anything could lift me up into the air, it would be Ellington!

That's for sure! But what about Reinhardt and music?

Well, I would never think of telling him to try his hand in music because he was so busy doing what he was doing. He was totally focused on his painting, so it was best not to distract him.

What about yourself? Did you play an instrument?

I monkeyed with the drums and clarinet.

Were you good?

I guess I provided a lot of entertainment. (Laughter).

Spiral Dream Yoga

In addition to your musical interests, I know you like to draw. Hasn't some of your artwork been published along with your poems?

Sure, I've done drawings and sketches…

Yes, and your letters to me usually include a little sketch or design or some multicoloured configuration of dots. You most often make use of yellow, blue, and red tones.

It's great fun to draw, and I like the primary colours, the basic tones where everything else begins.

Has your art gone on exhibit?

Some drawings and poem prints have gone on tour to Stuttgart, Florence, and other places.

Were you an artistic "late bloomer"?

I did art in college, at least I certainly did cartoons. I think I was doing various kinds of drawings too, zip-zap drawings.

Zip-zap drawings?

Drawings that are quick, spontaneous, going with the flow.

You still do them, don't you?

Sure, all the time. Sometimes they take the place of writing. If ever you feel like just letting it all out, whatever "it" might be, I say do a zip-zap sketch. Look, here's one.

It looks like an energetic spiral. You like drawing spirals. Why?

I just like things that spiral up and down. I like the fact that spirals are circles but not closed circles. You can keep on going with a spiral. You can go all the way around but still keep going and going with the flow.

You sound a little like Reinhardt with his love of things circular.

(Laughter). Friends oftentimes express similar sentiments.

That spiral stuff also subtly sounds like the DNA-RNA arrangement. You know, the double-helix, that kind of thing.

I'm not a geneticist, but that's certainly a good insight.

Or it could be a bedspring.

(Laughter). How did you come to think of a bedspring – just because I'm lying on one right now?

Yeah – spiral dream yoga.

Now that sounds like one of those newfangled ice creams! You're in top form today, old boy. Keep it swirling up, up and up!

Speaking of things that go around and around, and I'm not talking about frosties, the Greek philosopher Pythagoras[7] said that to live well, you have to learn how to join the end with the beginning.

Who?

Pythagoras. The guy down the block over on the isle of Samos. You know him, Bob.

Oh, yes. Pythagoras. He was a good boy.

(Laughter). Just as an aside, did you know that some scholars theorize that he may have given his disciples opium?

I see, I see. Do go on, tell me more.

And through the influence of opium, that's how they heard the "Music of the Spheres"![8]

Did they put him in the clink for that?

No, I don't think so.

Well, that's a relief.

(Laughter). Now what about Pythagoras' statement, "To live well, you have to join the end with the beginning"?

I like it.

Yes, but what do you think?

I don't really know, Steve. It sounds true enough, but I don't know what he had in mind.

Maybe he had nature's cycles in mind. The pre-Socratic philosophers studied the environment. Perhaps he saw how winter becomes spring.

That's quite possibly true.

Do you have anything else to say about Pythagoras?

(Laughter). $a^2 + b^2 = c^2$

Oh well, I guess we'd better leave old Pythagoras alone for a while. Maybe it's time to move on, Bob.

If that's OK with you, but I don't want to rush you. I mean, I remember you're the fellow who sent me fifty postcards in a two-month span, most of them featuring wild motorcycles. You might get miffed and do it again, Brother Harley!

But Bobo, that was all in jest!

I know, I know. And from one jester to another, let's rev up our rockets and blast off!

Right on, Dreamcatcher, Uncle Zoomer, Supercool Starman of Zowie! Our Astrobikes are geared for action! (Laughter). So tell me, have you ever stopped to think that wherever you go, you are drawn toward artistic circles, or, as in a number of places, they seem to form around you? Artists from all over the world have spent time with you, and you with them, and you've had great times together. I think this has much to do with the inspiration and good vibes that you give. Like you've said, art should be a harmonizer, a peacemaker, and that's exactly what you are!

Well, that's good to hear. At least I'm doing something right.

No, really. So many artists have come here to meet you and to work here, and they have felt totally blessed to be with you. Some even sense you to be the centre of this spiritually creative arena.

(Laughter). Thanks, but right now I just want to go under a stone somewhere.

When will you ever stop being so hyper-humble?

Come on now, it's not so bad to be humble. That "humus" in humility means earth. When we touch the earth, we can't help to grow, all in God's good time. So it's good to be humble, as long as your humility is not grounded in drawing attention to yourself.

OK. And it's good to be wise, too.

And compassionate.

And kind.

And loving.

And thanksgiving.

Right, right, right! But if you are really going to say thanks, believe me, it ends up taking a whole lifetime.

And that's exactly what you have been doing.

(Laughter). I have every reason to do so. I'm just trying to be a good boy.

And you're not finished saying "thank you."

No, I'm not.

You've only just begun.

Like I do every day, son.

You know, a long time ago, perhaps the very night that I met you, you told me, "When you create, don't create for someone or something – create for God and His angels." Why did you say this?

Well, earlier you brought up the philosopher Pythagoras, which was great. I like him, I really do. All that circular stuff is wonderful, and the meanings are infinite, involving life now, and in the hereafter. But did you know that the pre-Socratic Empedocles said, "God is a centre whose circle is everywhere and whose circumference is nowhere?" So, no matter where you go, what you do, you're always in the presence of God. He is your Audience.

Yes, that reminds me of the time a few years ago when I was washing our dinner dishes in the kitchen and you called out from the other room. "Steve, where are you?" you asked. And I replied, "I'm in the kitchen." Then you said, "No, try again." So I said, "I'm in your house." And you answered, "Sorry – one more try." And I said, "I'm on Patmos," and for the third time I was wrong.

And then I walked over to the kitchen and what did I tell you?

That you and I and all things are forever in the presence of God.

[1] Robert Lax. *A Thing That Is: New Poems,* edited by Paul Spaeth. New York: Overlook, 1997.

[2] *PAX,* a short-lived artist-writer publication founded by Lax in 1955. It was Lax's hope that this peace-promoting paper would eventually benefit people all over the world, especially the sick and those in prison. Lax felt that through art and poetry peace could become a greater reality. Contributors to PAX included Jack Kerouac, E.E. Cummings, and Ernesto Cardenal. Interestingly, the last manuscript Lax wrote prior to his death was *The Peacemaker's Handbook.* This book, the passages of which were selected by Judith Emery and edited by Michael Daugherty, was published by Pendo-Verlag and released in September 2001.

[3] Cine Nomad of Munich, under the direction of Nicholas Humbert and Warner Penzel, has also made *Middle of the Moment,* 1995, an award-winning film in which Lax is featured.

[4] The Zen master D.T. Suzuki was a good friend of Thomas Merton. Through Suzuki, Merton (and many theologians, artists, and writers of the West, such at Alan Watts and Jack Kerouac) learned a good deal about Zen and the Zen arts. See Merton's *Zen And The Birds Of Appetite,* 1968.

[5] See *A Catch of Anti-letters,* edited by Thomas Merton, Kansas City, MO: Sheed & Ward, 1978.

[6] Lax would write about the Afro-American jazz artist Sun Ra (1914–1993): *Sun Ra: Notes and Numbers,* 1984.

[7] Pythagoras of Samos (sixth century BC) is probably the most famous of the Greek philosophers before Socrates. Although well known for his geometrical theorem, he was primarily a philosopher and mystic who utilized numbers to discover divine truths said to be existent in the cosmos. Other well known pre-Socratics include Heraclitus, Thales, Parmenides, and Empedocles. For more on the pre-Socratics, see *Early Greek Philosophy,* Jonathan Barnes. London: Penguin Books, 1987 and

The Pythagorean Sourcebook, compiled and translated by K.S. Guthrie, Grand Rapids, MI: Phanes Press, 1987.

[8] The "Music of the Spheres" refers to a Pythagorean belief that a celestial "music" could be heard chiming in the heavens if one had reached a certain level of purity and receptivity. This purification was actualized through diet, exercise, contemplation, and the study of geometry. Pythagoras believed that all things in the cosmos were so perfectly proportioned that the ecstasy of that proportion echoed in the heavens, and those that likened themselves to this "cosmic harmony" eventually came to hear the "Music of the Spheres."

"Prayer is a way of sending out love everywhere
at once." Lax in prayer.

"We're like little lights meant to guide each other home." Votive candles burn in the Monastery of St. John the Theologian.

Robert Lax and the author walk the lengthy concrete pier in Skala, the port town of Patmos. Here the poet would routinely take meditative strolls.

"The sunlight writes on the water, and the waters wave in the light." Sunrise from the Monastery of St. John the Theologian.

"We'll always be walking and talking together."

"This is a place of crossings where time's spiral has carved a deep well..." (from "A Song for Our Lady," by Robert Lax). The author at the grave of Robert Lax, situated in the Friar's Cemetery, near St. Bonaventure University, New York. The poet lies not far from the pasture known as "Merton's Heart," where Thomas Merton used to pray before he took monastic vows and entered the Abbey of Gethsemani.

Fishing boat bearing the name St. Petros (Peter) in the harbour of Skala, Patmos. "In another land and with my own compass, I will not look further for righteousness; I will understand you only in your absences" (from *Journal C* by Robert Lax).

Moschos Lagouvardos, 1995.

Robert Lax (1915–2000)

SPIRIT

Sometimes we go on a search
And we do not know what we are looking for,
Until we come again to our beginning…

Robert Lax,
from *Circus of the Sun*

Though Lax writes in an unmistakably spiritual framework, his Christian ethos does not openly manifest itself because it may be said that he creates in an "interfaith manner." His minimalist verse, so steeped in the love of all things, takes on many levels of interpretation and appreciation. Yet it must be understood that at the core of his craft, the Christian message of love, wisdom, and power quietly predominates.

Like a true spiritual master, Lax the poet does not point to himself but to the sacrosanct beauty of creation which, through its graced existence, exquisitely praises the Creator: "Ever since the creation of the world, His invisible nature, namely, His eternal power and deity, has been clearly perceived in the things that have been made" (Romans 1.20). In turning his reader's attention to the praise songs of the cosmos, to creation "making a poem of itself," Lax consciously reduces his manifold powers of expression to a bare minimum and through sparse, ascetic verse lets nature teach its fundamental, theocentric lessons. In this way, Lax echoes the kenotic nature of John the Baptist, who had humbly effaced himself before Jesus: "He must increase, and I must become the lesser" (John 3.30). Just as John functioned as an obedient and vocal witness to Christ, so the poet Lax acts as a faithful witness to the presence of God in nature and humanity.

In *The White Bird*,¹ we see Lax at his minimalist best:

the
white
bird

the
white
bird

the
dark
hill

the
dark
hill

the
white
bird

the
white
bird

the
dark
sea

the
dark
hill

the
dark
hill

the
white
bird

the
white
bird

the
white
bird

the
white
bird

the
dark
sea

Here the "dark hill" and the "dark sea" are contrasted with the wheeling "white bird," which flies a circular, rhythmic course amidst a tight linear background. A subtle and at times pulsating tension dominates the selection, indicating how the ethereal white bird is on the verge of transcending the darkness of the poem's taut form and setting. In essence, the salvation of the Spirit, represented by the white bird wheeling in mid-heaven, is about to descend and alight upon a darkened world. Yet at the same time, this stirring visual scene, presented in a very innocent and childlike way, may simply be taken at face value; there is a dark hill, a dark sea, and a wheeling white bird, all of which are beautiful, mysterious and dreamlike in themselves. The purity of the images and their basic, honest form stimulates meditation in the reader. And if the poem is read mindfully, reverently, one is left with a feeling of awe, if not ominous wonder. A type of holy contemplation is effected, using all but a few quiet words. Yet as both kabbalistic and Eastern wisdom profess, only a minimum of words are necessary to create a mystical experience, for even the very letters of words embody spiritual power. Therefore when Lax's poems are read with open eyes and heart, their finely crafted blessings are liberated and radiate out to infinity.

It is into this "infinite holy space" that Lax – much like the poet-mystic St. John of the Cross – projects his readers. Using primal, nature-based imagery, Lax leads his audience from the simple and familiar to the dark and unknowable mystery of God. As Lax intones, this almighty and descriptionless Being is perhaps best revealed in sparse, ascetic verse, which, in its sheer transparency and depth, ultimately gives way to the "empty space" of the illimitable Spirit.

Just Love

Roberto! This morning I was up at the Monastery of St. John, and I met a man named Manolis who asked that I relay his greetings to you. He said he's an old friend from Kalymnos.

Oh yes, Manolis – one of my fisherman friends. Well, that's great! You tell him I said hello too, and give him my very best.

He also added that you are an "aghios anthropos," a holy man.

Oh, well, that's good to know, too. Tell him he's just as holy as I am. (Laughter). What's up for today?

The spiritual dimension.

I thought we were already there.

That's true. But we're going to get a little more in-depth. And I'd like to start by asking you about your transit into the afterlife.

(Laughter). Well, that's certainly cutting to the chase, as they say. What is it that you want to know? Do you really think I can give you an answer?

Let's say heaven officially found you to be a very good man and you went on up to the realm of the blessed...

Yes? Keep going.

If you had the opportunity to come back down to earth and help others get there as well, would you do it?

Now is that what you were wondering about? Well, certainly I would. And as far as you and I go, don't worry – we'll always be walking and talking together, strolling up and down that old harbour.

So you are a Catholic Bodhisattva?[2]

(Laughter). Is that what that amounts to? Let's let heaven decide! What else is up?

In our past walks and talks together, you've mentioned that there's value in listening to "angel voices." Are you talking about intuition here, or do you really mean that we should be listening for angels?

I think I'm talking about intuition.

But at the same time, Merton actually heard angel voices, or so he writes in The Seven Storey Mountain.

Yes, he did. I believe it happened to him a few times. Well, if I heard an angel voice that I felt could not be attributed to intuition, I'd quietly listen and weigh what had been said. If I was still baffled by what I heard, I'd go find a good spiritual director and talk it over.

So the possibility of hearing an actual angel voice is there?

Oh yes, it's always there. But just be sure it's an angel's voice.

What else could it be?

Delusion, for one thing.

What about a dark force? Do you believe in a negative power that tries to instigate evil and captivate humanity?

I believe that there is one supreme force – if force is what you want to call it – and that is the force of God's love. That is what endures and prevails. When I get a sniff of dualism, I say that's not for me. In a way, the dark is there to help the light, and the light is there to help the dark.

How so?

Ideally, the errors of the unjust man should inspire feelings of compassion and forgiveness in the just man, and so the just man – the one who knows better – freely gives of his goodness to his unjust brother. In this way, the just man serves as an impartial and consistent model of love. He doesn't judge – he only loves.

What about the devil?

Well, I'm not saying that Lucifer, as an angel of God, does not exist. That would be wrong. He is an angel who fell from grace, and he has his role to play as the Accuser whose mission it is to fault us before God. But to think that there are good and evil forces endlessly at war in the universe is not for me. I'd rather focus on *love*. Love builds bridges, not walls. Anyway, I remember somebody saying, "Even if there is a devil, he still remains God's devil."

I've also heard it said that Lucifer is not completely at fault in his fall from grace because he didn't know what he was doing – it was his enormous pride which blinded him. He therefore made an irrational decision, and his self-obsession continues to obscure his judgment.

I don't know what exactly was going on when Lucifer fell, but I do know that good spiritual counsel tells us that we should refrain from judging even him, lest we too become proud. However evil Lucifer may have become, he still remains one of God's creatures. Perhaps his continued existence may also have to do with testing our capacity to forgive. Certainly for those who injure us, we should pray for them all the more. I think it was St. Isaac of Syria who said that we should pray for all creatures, for people, animals, reptiles, even for the enemies of God. One who loves can't bear the thought that anything in creation is suffering.

Yes, I guess if you truly love, you love all, and in the process, you don't judge. This reminds me of a story from the Desert Fathers.[3]

Go on.

A desert father was asked by a demon, "Who are the lambs and who are the goats?" The father replied, "The goats are sinners like myself, but who the lambs are, only God knows." Thus the father did not break the commandment "Do not judge."

Yes, that's good. Now I don't know if this helps at all, but like Mircea Eliade,[4] I do believe that Christianity may be likened to an evolutionary spiral. In fact, I think that all people of all religions are evolving and are meant to evolve as they spiral toward a holy infinity. This infinity is heaven, and from what we hear about it, the evolution continues even there. There are signs of this evolution in every world religion, and any religion that tries to stop this inborn spiritual evolution gets stopped in its own tracks. Like it or not, the flow continues.

But what about those people who don't do enough self-discovery, and perhaps as a result of that, resist the flow and commit evil acts? Do you think that they don't enter paradise?

Ultimately, I think everyone evolves into something better. A terrible act – once recognized – can be the first step in righting oneself. It is a self-taught lesson. As they say, "stumbling blocks can become stepping stones." Eventually, there's no place to go, really, but the right place, the place where love calls you. Love calls all things back to a blessed beginning of some sort. As long as there is life, there always exists the potential to do good.

How does this fit in with Catholic teaching? Doesn't the Catholic Church believe in heaven and hell?

And purgatory too.

Yes. So are you practising a more eclectic form of Catholicism? Don't you think that your views may be too liberal?

No, I don't think so. I am a Roman Catholic who feels that anything in which we believe has much to do with a hybrid of influences that stem from childhood. And my way of looking at hell, for instance, is that you really have to choose to be in hell. You've got to say, "This is where I really want to be, this is where the nice warm fires are." So if an angel comes to you when you're in hell and states, "How about repenting now?" and you refuse to do so, well, I guess that's where you'd better stay. But I love people too much to imagine that anyone would want to stay in hell forever, even if we will always have free will unto eternity.

This brings to mind yet another story from the Desert Fathers having to do with heaven and hell. It relates to heaven and hell being one, and not two realms. Essentially, only the realm of God's love exists. This blessed love manifests itself as an almighty fire. The fire warms the loving faithful, but burns those who are unloving and faithless. It's still the same singular holy fire; however, its ability to warm or burn depends upon the natures of those who react with it.

That's wonderful, so insightful. I can certainly relate to that description.

After hearing your views about heaven and hell, I guess that "good" and "bad" are relative terms for you. To paraphrase Shakespeare, "Nothing is really good or bad; only thinking makes it so."

To me, they are not real opposites because the situation in which "good" and "evil" come into play is also important. What might be "good" in this moment could be "bad" in another. Of course, when I periodically say "good," as in the completion of a task or something well done, that is a nurturing response born of love.

If "good" and "bad" are always in flux, how do we ride the change from a perceived good to a perceived bad and then to a perceived good again?

You are riding those changes from moment to moment. I remember an old Buddhist's sutra which imparted how in a single second there are hundreds and hundreds of moments. In essence, all we are really doing is riding the flow as lovingly and as compassionately and as patiently as we can. You know, a lot of spiritual study and training teaches one how to deal with each moment as it comes along. There is a holiness to the moment at hand. So it comes down to taking care of the moment. You respond to the needs of the moment as keenly as possible. Sometimes you can do this only by sounds – there are some moments when that is the very best response you can make.

Oh, so that's why every so often I hear you making unusual sounds, little sounds, sometimes happy, sometimes hinting of struggle. Then when I look at you, you break into a smile.

(Laughter). Could be, could be. But just try and take care of each moment, and if you do, you might wind up taking care of all time. Everything is happening *right now.*

Staying on Track

What is the best way to begin understanding the nature and texture of the moment?

First of all, it may help to keep in mind three things: there's God, you, and the moment, and every moment is like a gift. And since it is, then relax, get into the moment, and do all you can to listen to it. I mean, really, really listen. Be present to the moment with everything you are. It takes practice. After you've listened for a while, you start responding. I think you start working your gifts in response to what you've heard. You become appreciative of the moment. You give back because you begin to see how everything is on loan – a gift from God. I believe we will be held accountable for the gifts given us – that is, if we cultivated them or not.

What are you listening for?

Everything. In every moment there are so many sounds. And there are sounds within the sounds, deeper things happening, maybe one sound sounding in the whole of life, a kind of loving sound, whether from an ant or a star. But sometimes there's too much static, so I wait for things to clear…

Like when we're strolling down at the dock and then all of a sudden a Harley Davidson goes roaring by?

Oh yeah, you said it, brother, all that boomin' and zoomin' – to that I say *no thanks!* No, no, I most like tuning into sounds that might hearken to the quiet in Eden. And it's not a quiet roaring out for attention. It just is there, like a sea breeze or falling rain. I like listening to the wind too. Things that point toward that "still small voice." I mean, everything just seems to roll off of that voice, that is, if you are receptive to it.

It's amazing how you are so attentive. How does one learn to be attentive?

By being attentive. (Laughter). You've got to keep your mind on what you're doing.

Yes, you always talk about "being on the beam," "staying on track." But how do you do it?

Try listening, looking. Learn how to look; that is, take the time to see what's right there in front of you. Not to search around for what's there, just to let what you see sink in. When you look at a flower opening or a tree moving with the wind, you just relax and take it all in. Try and see everything like that, if you can. Yes, looking and listening lead into everything else. Real listening means you don't project yourself into the situation. You simply are receptive, seeing things as they are, not as you might wish them or imagine them to be. It's like starting out seeing a tree, but eventually you see both the tree and every leaf. You come to hear one sound and all sounds.

You become more totally aware of reality. It's so true — everything we need to live well is already within our possession. Wisdom is right before our very eyes.

Yes, but how exactly do we keep from weaving in our own imaginings and desires when we see someone or something?

You might just keep on looking. After a while, you might rethink your first impressions. Just continue being mindful. If we looked and listened more carefully, if we were truly mindful of everything we did, all of our actions would come to approximate blessings. Certainly reverberating blessings do flow from any job well done, especially if the entire act is accomplished with the whole of one's being.

Isn't that why people who assiduously work at a craft for a long time — whether it's weaving nets or plowing the field or working a loom — impart a feeling of refreshing calm? Their movements are magical, demonstrating how everyday tasks can transform into transcendent realities.

Yes, that's good. There's a shoemaker down the street who does excellent work, so rhythmic and wonderful. And on the side, he writes aphorisms which have to do with the blessings of work and its holy character.

Do you think that the meditative, transcendental possibilities inherent in manual labor have been overlooked by society?

You know, a lot has been written lately about the sacred manifesting itself in everyday tasks. The acts of sweeping the floor and putting out the garbage uphold the cosmos in their own way, and can help attain individual enlightenment and communal peace.

That reminds me of a saying: "Jesus wasn't mistaken for a theologian, but he was for a gardener."

Yes, that's it! One never knows in what form an enlightened man or enlightenment may come. What's more, it may well be the "work behind the work" which can help to make any job transfiguring – in other words, just pay careful attention to what it is that you are doing. Keep on paying attention. Like many wise folk have said, depth of practice produces wisdom. I mean, all you can do is what you are doing now, in this very moment. That's why you've got to use as much wisdom as you can in every moment. I keep on saying it's good to use all the radar you got to help you make the right choices and develop your being to the fullest. If you learn to do this regularly, I think you will be more aware of where you are and where you're headed. You'll better glimpse the person you were created to be. And do this slowly. Take small steps. What's your hurry, anyway? The journey is forever. Like St. Irenaeus said, "God will always have something more to teach us, and we will always have something more to learn from God."

All right, but do you feel that intense meditative practice actually prepares one for a mystical experience, for a type of illumination or revelation? Pascal said something like, "Grace favours the prepared mind."

I guess if you do your homework, it won't hurt. All good thoughts and intentions and deeds add up, no matter how insignificant. And, of course, a little bit of heaven can be glimpsed in every pure work. But, at the same time, I've heard it said that the Spirit blows where it will.

Yes, anything can happen; spiritual activity transcends human wisdom.

On that you can rely.

But say I am illumined; once I reach a state of heightened rapture, is thought really necessary?

Hello? What's that?

Well, perhaps all thought and meditation simply lead to mystical bliss — from a state of "doing" we enter a state of "being."

(Nearby church bells start ringing). I think those ecstatic moments of pure receptivity are unpredictable moments, moments of grace. At certain times you may indeed experience such extrasensory, transcendent states, but then you get back to where you were before. A kind of "levelling" takes place.

You know, it's interesting how those bells are ringing now that we are speaking about receptivity and bliss. As soon as I heard them, I really became more serene and happy — they are saying much more than words can.

Yes, it sure is amazing how things just seem to happen here. But the bells will stop, and you will be left with your thoughts.

So then how would you define lasting enlightenment?

I think it is when you come to see that the greatest thing you can do in this life is to cultivate and exercise compassion. Life is about learning how to flow with your basic goodness. It's about entering the heart and making it the fount of your being. What do the Proverbs say? "As a man thinketh in his heart, so he is."[5] Enlightenment is not about mesmerizing people or demonstrating power or revelling in a cocoon of isolated joy. First you come to see where you are in the world, where others are, and then you begin to take care of all things that come your way, as many as you can. It's good to gather the scattered things of the world and bring them into a kind of happy, loving communion. When you're doing that, you're well on the road to real illumination.

Turn Jungle into Garden

What meditation or awareness system do you practise?

Like I've said before, I freestyle. Sure I do yoga and breathing exercises and things like that, but anything can be a form of meditation, and I think you know that. But whatever you do, be sure to gather your mind in a quiet, peaceful way. Make it still like the surface of a pool so you can deal tranquilly with situations that come your way. Pretty soon your mind will go back to its natural, mindful state. That's why the mind is called "mind" in the first place – it "minds," it's meant to keep watch, sort of like Confucius said. Yes, anything you do, if it's done mindfully, can be calming, centring. Making dinner and washing dishes can be wonderful ways of learning how to be present to the moment.

Is that why whenever I eat with you the food tastes so good?

No...the island air works up your appetite, that's all.

Are you sure? I remember there was one time in the kitchen when you asked me to taste the soup you were stirring. My hands were full of dishes, so I bent down and you spoon-fed me. Man, the taste of that broth was exquisite! I tasted all the fields of the island.

Must have been the local vegetables or something – everything tastes better here, you know that. (Laughter).

Yeah, but you're some sort of super-chef, too.

Gee! And all this time I thought that I just had a good blender.

(Laughter). Robo, for someone your age, you seem to see so clearly and you have so much vitality. How do you cultivate your energy?

By now you should know where it comes from – it comes from "up there" (motioning upward). Everybody's does. And it's worked through prayer, meditation, creativity, exercising of gifts. Every moment in life is a prayer, or could be. I think you can pray yourself into the mystery of the moment, or allow for the blessings of the moment to sustain you. Every moment is an invitation, and whatever you do in that moment, if it's dedicated to God, then it is a prayer.

But do you have to dedicate your work to God? Can't you just do the work?

I definitely think that the dedication helps. Sometimes, though, too many words get in the way. Just be concise, to the point, and let your actions speak for themselves. You know, we are faced with choices every moment of our life. There are all kinds of choices in every phase of existence. Even if you are folding a napkin, you can fold it correctly in a balanced manner or be careless and fold it without concern. Your real work is to make each choice as best you can. Do your utmost in every moment. Don't go back and waste your energy focusing on past mistakes. If you focus on the "now-moment" and devote yourself to it with all your heart, you will not be far off from being the saint you were called to be.

And since God is present in every moment, we are called to sense His presence.

Yes, truly. Certainly one thing that I think can help us become more aware of the divine presence is proper breathing, which is so vital physically and spiritually.

Adam became a living being through the breath of God.

That's right – breath is spirit, life. People who advocate that we should breathe properly know that our levels of awareness are heightened through good breathing. Right breathing can help steady a restless heart and keep one focused. Truly, every breath is a rebirth – we breathe out the old and breathe in the new. We should breathe from the soles of our feet in a slow, calm, blossoming way, then push out the breath in the fullest possible manner, but always slowly, gently. If singing or background music helps in doing this, then that's a good thing also. Singing or listening to nice, easy, restful music is healthy for you, anyway. It soothes every cell in the body. Those good vibrations get right into every atom.

If people cultivate their God-centred energy throughout their lives, do you feel that when they get old and start losing their physical and mental powers, the inner light that they have exercised over the years starts to shine out of them?

Oh yes, I do believe that! And it's never too late to work the spirit.

So do you think that one of the primary goals of spiritual labour is the cultivation of this "light energy"?

I think we are here to find out who we are both as individuals and as a collective, interdependent people, all under God. In the process, we pray, we learn to think through the heart, and we do many other things that can make this a greater reality. That light stuff happens by itself along the way.

But why are we drawn toward wisdom? We could just simply exist, yet there seems to be an inborn need to investigate life, to order it, and to make living more comfortable and meaningful.

We are drawn to wisdom because it's part of the flow. It's organic! We are drawn in that direction for the very same reason why cats and dogs and the whole of life is drawn toward wisdom — we need it, just like oxygen. It's where we are going, as we are going. It's our path which is the way of the heart. I think that the Latin root of "educate" has to do with "leading out." I believe we're all on a journey of self and communal discovery. It's all about turning a jungle into a garden —

"Without destroying a single flower," as you say.

Good.

Now, can you tell me how you determine if someone is spiritually alive?

Isn't that up to God?

Yes, but simply by looking at someone, how do you evaluate their spiritual state?

214

I don't know what kind of answer you're looking for, but when I look at someone, what gets my attention is not their face. I usually don't quite remember it. What registers for me are the eyes – I look at the light in the eyes, the quality, clearness, and lucidity of the eyes. Eyes seem so much like microgalaxies, like big bangs of life.

Maybe that's why we come alive when we meet the gaze of someone who loves us. It's been said that the eyes are the windows of the soul.

Oh yes, in many ways I think that's true.

There's a story I've heard about your eyes. They used to be a hazel brown, but now they're most often a very clear blue. Did you get contact lenses?

Naw…first I better trim my beard before I do that! (Laughter). You see, what happened was that my eyes changed colour when I came to Greece. They really did because documents from my pre-Patmos days indicate that I had darker eyes. I thought maybe the sea and the intense light here may have changed them, but a doctor friend said that it naturally happens to some people when they get old.

You can't be old! Last night along the beach, Ulf [6] and I were talking about your incredibly keen senses, especially how clear and sharp your eyes are. We're going to call you Laser! I remember how once when you and I were walking near the main town, you picked up a buried needle right out of the sandy road because you worried that a child might step on it. How did you see it?

(Laughter). Oh, yes…well, I just did. But our artist friend Ulf, he's really visually gifted. He takes notice of how everything looks, doesn't miss a detail. He had a nice show in town over the summer. Niko and Vito did too.

Right. Ulf's getting ready now for the arts exhibition that will be going on in Skala in celebration of the millennium.

Yes, he's been coming up here and keeping me informed. It's going to be a good event, I think. I look forward to hearing more about it.

A Son of Israel

Robert, sometimes when we're walking along the shore, the Greek men sitting along the waterfront point to you and me and make gestures of approval. They consider you a wise man and encourage my being in your company. And writers like Jack Kerouac, James Uebbing, William Maxwell, Brother Patrick Hart, Julian Mitchell, Alexander Eliot, and others have referred to you as something of a "mystic" — even the word "saint" has been repeatedly used.[7] People feel happy in your presence and are naturally attracted to you. You've steered many in good directions, and you like doing that. Even your zany letters make people feel strangely glad. Merton himself wrote of how spiritually advanced you were, more so than himself. What do you have to say about all of this?

(Laughter). You're not giving up, are you? I don't know what to say. I really can't say that I've thought about it, not for a second. Sure, I do have a natural tendency to move toward the spiritual, and if Merton thought the same, that's wonderful. I think that I was most myself when I was with him, and if that's what Merton thought, why should I doubt him? I just keep on trying to be a good boy, that's all.

Yes, but since your youth so many people have made comments about your spiritual gifts. I remember reading of how Catherine Doherty, the Director of Friendship House in Harlem, referred to you as a "son of Israel in whom Love spoke loudly in every gesture." You were only in your twenties then!

Well, yes, she wrote that. But you can't gag everybody, now, can you? (Laughter). Whatever Catherine and others have seen in me is not of my own making, but is a gift. Clearly, I did say my prayers devoutly and as consciously as I could from the time that I was a child, and from an early age I felt a spiritual calling…but you know, Uncle Steve, one thing's for sure.

What's that?

You give me faith that heaven is directing people to my door for some good and sustaining purpose.

Wow! Do you realize that you have said more about your natural predisposition to charity in the last few minutes than anything I've heard over the years? You've always been so modest, right from the start. Way back when I met you in 1993, you never exactly revealed who you were, just that you were a poet named Lax, and that I should read Thomas Merton. So when I returned to San Francisco and did some homework, that's when I discovered how everything fit together!

(Laughter). Yes, I do remember your first impromptu visit…

Even now you're pointing away from yourself! You're hiding behind your walking staff which you've positioned right in front of you, and it's casting a shadow over your face –

My "staff," did you say? This ain't no staff – it's a stick, and don't you forget it!

(Laughter). OK, Zen master. I'll back off. I don't want to go to the beat-up room.

Darn right you don't, Brother Knucklehead! Want me to zap your zop? This place is especially set up to take care of wild ones like you! (Laughter). Really, though, Steve, what's surprising about all those honorific things that have been said about me is that they are so meaningless. I mean, sure, if I were to describe myself as an active or contemplative, I would be obliged to say contemplative. But I don't say this in any grand sense. I don't go about as though caught up in a revelation. I just love looking out the window – I love to contemplate the scene. I like to look at the ships and the sky, the mountains and the sea, the stars and the moon. In that sense, contemplation is just a normal act.

Yes, but with all due respect you know that you have a profound gift for nurturing and healing. I've heard stories here on Patmos of how *you've helped out lots of people over the years in many different ways. You've come to the aid of those who were searching, depressed, unable to go on in life. And even as a child you sought to help your peers. When you were quite young you dreamed that you had saved the children about you from falling and hurting themselves by holding up a banister that had broken in a school hallway.*

Son, how can I answer you? About that dream, that's true – I did have that dream. But you know that everything is based upon love. I truly believe that loving people is a basic part of my nature. *I do love people.* One reason I'm glad that I was born is that I wouldn't have been able to meet the people that I've met. And I think I developed these feelings of compassion through my father, who set the right example for me. He really loved people and introduced me to lots of folk – real people like truck drivers, fishermen, cooks, carpenters, gardeners – whom I met and spoke with every day. It's rare that I don't like someone. I'm really conscious of it, though, and if that feeling should come up, I try and work on my dislike in one way or another. Maybe I try to pray for them more, or be extra nice to them, whatever is necessary to try and eradicate the negative feeling.

Did you experience these feelings of dislike for "Microbe Man"?[8]

Right! Right! You know what I mean – oh, yes, Microbe Man! (Laughter). But really, and I can't say it enough, I believe that we were created to love, and everything else was created to make love possible. Love holds everything in place. Love listens, and understands how everything should be dealt with patiently, overarchingly; it takes in the whole, and not just the part. I think it was St. John of the Cross who said that when we go "up there," we will be quietly asked, "What did you love?"

You know, while coming over to Greece on the airplane I read a great quote from Teilhard de Chardin which I wrote in my notebook — here it is: "Someday, after mastering the waves and the wind, we shall harness for God the energy of love; and then, for the second time in human history, we will have discovered Fire."[9]

That's just great. Really, so wonderful.

Acquire the Spirit of Peace

What does Jesus mean to you?

Jesus tells me to love. He doesn't tell me to hate or to kill – He tells me to love. What appeals to me most about Jesus is His role as the Prince of Peace. Peace is really one of the key words in all that concerns me now. I'm highly enamoured of the saying by that beloved Russian Orthodox saint, Seraphim of Sarov: "Acquire the Spirit of Peace, and thousands around you will be saved."[10]

Yes, you have those lines pasted up there on your "reading and viewing wall," and you say them to me every time I see you.

More and more, I'm very much emphasizing the power of peace. So many good and lasting things proceed from peace. I get a clear feeling about this sort of thing. You shouldn't fight fire with fire; you address fire with water. And the water is *agape*, *ahimsa*,[11] non-violence... I mean, cruel people are still people, but they have somehow forgotten how to love. Being cruel to them will only reinforce their cruelty. But what might kindness do? What might peacefulness do? I think that's what Jesus was thinking about...

You associate peace and love with Jesus, but what about Mary? How do you perceive the Madonna's role in the Church? Is she a real or symbolic figure for you?

Mary is symbolic of life, birth, and growth. At the same time, I also feel that Mary is an intercessory figure. That's her mission, that's why she was born.

Are we all intercessory beings?

I think we are all potentially intercessory beings. We are all meant to be. I believe that Mary would want us to be life-saving beings, and nurturers. And we begin to do this by being peaceful. You know, some of the monks here give a nice greeting: *Eirini Pahsi* ("Peace Be Unto All"). I like that.

Speaking of the monks, I've always wondered how you practise Catholicism on a distinctly Eastern Orthodox island. What about Mass and taking regular Communion?

At times, I attend the Orthodox services and pray in the churches here. I think the liturgies are tranquil, beautiful. I remember when Merton died, one of the first things I did was to go into a church in which I had often prayed... As for Mass and Communion, every so often Father Peter, a Franciscan from Rhodes, comes over and conducts a Catholic Mass on the isle, and I take Communion from him. But you know, any place where you love and care and pray for another becomes something like a church.

With regard to your relations with the Orthodox on the island, there was a holy man of Patmos who died in 1970 named Amphilochius Makris, a monk whom many Patmians feel will be the next canonized saint of the Greek Orthodox Church.[12] *During the latter years of his life and since his death, miracles have been attributed to him. Did you know this monk?*

He was truly a wonderful man. He had a great love of nature, and especially loved trees – he called them "vertical prayers to God." I remember there was one day when I went to the Sunday liturgy at the Monastery of the Annunciation[13] and he was officiating. He saw that I had no book to follow the service with so he came down from the altar and gave me a copy. If I had a say, I'd certainly vote for his canonization.

Having lived in the Orthodox East for nearly half a century, what Orthodox classics have you read and liked?

The Philokalia and *The Way of the Pilgrim* are both wonderful. I've also enjoyed St. John Climacus' *Ladder of Divine Ascent* and Archimandrite Sophrony's *The Monk of Mt. Athos*, in which Sophrony writes about his mentor, the Elder Silouan.[14]

So you have read many spiritual works exemplifying a wide range of traditions and have meditated and prayed extensively, but has it ever happened that your faith in God has waned?

Truly, I don't think it has. He's come to my rescue so many millions of times, and in lots of desperate situations – how could I dare to think so? To be without faith would be to lose everything. I love God, and, like St. John the Evangelist, I think that perfect love casts out fear. Love creates the perfect conditions for living. It's the basis for everything. I guess I have faith and I continue to hope because I love.

So it's faith, hope, and love. And do you know The Philokalia *states, "It is more serious to lose hope than to sin"?*

I believe in that wholeheartedly.

Still, though, you must get depressed or spiritually frustrated. What do you do?

I pray, maybe draw, go for a walk, or just think about what's going on. I listen more, that sort of thing. Sometimes when I'm not sure of something, I turn to the Bible. Or I might even open up the Bible three times and at random put my finger on a passage. This helps me to get a sense of direction.

Both St. Augustine and St. Francis did something like that.

Yes, well, I've found that I get good results, and it's helped me to focus on new things, peaceful things. Scripture can help to reorient you. You can better glimpse land on the horizon and may get a better sense of where your boat is going.

Learning with Pleasure

Captain Petros, I feel some cosmic questions coming on.

Well, my boy, you better ask them while you can. A wind's coming up, and we may well have to get back on deck.

(Laughter). As you command, sir! So now that the sea is still calm, tell me about the Second Coming — do you think that all shall take place as described in Revelation, or do you favour a more metaphysical interpretation of the Apocalypse?

One may say that the "Second Coming" is in every moment because in every moment Jesus can save. But I find that the Second Coming, as indicated in Scripture, is easy to believe and to hope for.

Do you believe that angels may walk the earth disguised as human beings?

Sure, just like St. Paul did.[15] There's always a connection with the divine going on. Let's not forget Jacob's Ladder, that ladder between heaven and earth by which angels descend and ascend.[16] There are messengers and messages everywhere. Maybe "up there" we'll see how everything relates a whole lot better.

Do you feel that in the next life we will also have a greater understanding of who we are? Are we like children in this life who are only learning how to walk?

Oh, I like what you just said, I really do. We're like children…

Yes?

Well, that's simply beautiful!

You know, it's interesting how as my questions get increasingly narrow in focus, your answers get more minimal as well! (Laughter). Oh, wait — here's something I never asked you. Have you ever seen any ghosts? Any demons or angels?

No, I can't say that I have, my boy.

Have you witnessed any miracles here on Patmos? The islanders say St. John's energy is working all the time.

No, I can't claim to have seen a miracle take place. But every day, every moment is a miracle. Daily we get a chance to renew ourselves, to make a brand new beginning.

The night skies of Patmos are so clear, so full of shooting stars. Have you ever seen a UFO up here or high atop Mt. Kastelli?

No, and no little green men, either!

(Laughter). Do you believe that life exists on other planets?

I tend to believe so, and I think that these alien life forms have their own ways of consciousness which are part of a greater super-consciousness in which we are included. The astronaut people I've met – and I have been to astronautical congresses in Europe and have friends associated with SETI (Search for Extraterrestrial Intelligence) and NASA like Jill Tartar and the moonwalker Buzz Aldrin – all seem to feel it's likely that life on other worlds exists. It's sort of like many stars, one sky.

How fascinating! I knew you had an interest in astronomy but never heard about your association with the astronauts and all that. I've called you "Starman" at times, and you really are!

Well, I wouldn't go that far, but early on, a friend of mine, Jim Harford,[17] took me to many astronautical congresses as a photographer for his scientific magazine. I've met and photographed astronauts and space technicians from various countries. We got along fine, and it didn't matter if they came from Russia, China, or Japan.

Wow – you've done so much! You've met so many interesting people!

But Steve, I wouldn't have had this particular experience if it weren't for my friend Jim, who, had he been at Columbia, would have certainly been part of our gang. I met him and his wife, Millie, in Paris when he was still an engineering student – he had just gotten married and was on his honeymoon. He's really a fantastic person, marvellously communicative, and has great diplomatic skills which he uses on the international scale with the Russians, Chinese, and others.

What else do you remember from your astronautical days?

I recall how the American astronauts were more like engineering students, whereas the Russian cosmonauts were romantic in what they saw in space and in the future of space travel. And I remember the faces of the astronauts who had been up there for a long time, and they had amazing, fulfilled faces...the same expression Padre Pio had after meditating.

So outer space and inner space are related?

Yes, up there the astronauts certainly had time to get into their inner space, all right! (Laughter). And they didn't get shocked by their return to life on earth – they all had smiling, beautiful faces. They had something happy to bring back and share.

What about friends you have known who have passed on — have these "voyagers of the hereafter" come back in some way to comfort you?

Well, friends who have died have certainly appeared to me in my dreams. We get back in touch. I dream of Merton often.

What types of dreams are these?

Nice and friendly dreams of various kinds. Especially in recent dreams, our communication has been closer than at any other point. I mean, he seems to be right here with me, and I'm always laughing with him.

It seems that you are always smiling and giggling. Way back in the fifties, Jack Kerouac called you "Laughing Buddha." Why is laughter so important to you?

I don't know if I would use the word "important," because I'm not always checking myself to make sure I'm doing it. But it's certainly natural.

Is laughter a release for you? Is it a way of telling others that you're happy, and that you encourage happiness in others?

I'm sure you can figure this out for yourself, but laughing does tend to relax you. The doctors say it's very good for you. Comics and clowns do a lot with it. If you see light dancing in someone's eyes, how can you not be happy and laugh?

So it's a way of saying everything is OK – I'm with you, and we're in this thing called life together?

I can see that. I think laughing calms down not just yourself, but whoever you're with. Call it wordless communication, wordless consolation. It's a kind of joyful communion that is universal.

Plato said that when we learn with pleasure, we learn full measure.

And Plato was right.

Waiting on God

What about signs? Do you believe that God makes His presence and/ or divine activity known through mystical indications?

I think everyone, at times, picks up on this. One thing that happens to me that might relate to what you're asking is that if I see someone who looks like a person I know, but isn't that person, the chances are pretty good that soon I'll see the person that I thought I had seen earlier. There's actually a special name for that psychic process, but I can't think of it now.

That's OK. Answer me this – how would you address this statement: "All the world's wisdom is not worth one dead child"?

Well, Steve, there's a ball from left field! I mean, who knows those things? I think I can feel what moved someone to say that, and it's a question that we are all going to take up with our Creator. We just have to keep on loving and hoping and praying and wait for His answer. Someday, everything will be heard right. In the meantime, let's keep the faith alive. We have to trust, no matter what, because deep down we know that life is ultimately stronger than death.

So we "wait upon God."

Yes, yes. I think the whole world is waiting on God, praising Him in the morning, keeping the faith through the night. Maybe every created thing is sort of asking the same question: "Why?" I think we'll one day find out – all in His good time. But in the meantime, let's not forget how it's love that keeps on holding everything together, even when things seem dark. Heaven still keeps on loving us in an abiding, always encouraging way. We just have to listen and be patient.

In your haunting and acclaimed 21 Pages, the idea of "waiting" is dominant. Writing in the first person, you seem to be endlessly waiting, a waiting that sounds as if you are ultimately waiting on the Almighty. Can you elaborate?

After coming to Greece, the question of who or what I was waiting for was getting narrowed down, in a sense. I had the time to turn it over in my mind. You see, from adolescence on, I found that waiting – waiting for someone to keep an appointment or any other kind of waiting like that – could be a painful process. But on the other hand, I found that it could serve as a time in which I could better come to know myself. So when I came to Greece, I would reflect upon all the thoughts and anxieties and impressions that had occurred to me while I was waiting through the years. It would be hard to do this if I had been running down the block in New York trying to catch an appointment, but now I had the opportunity to see things in a clearer light. What's interesting is that I discovered how the waiting process continued even out here. Over on Kalymnos, I used to wait for an old fellow who was my swimming companion, and there was no telling when he would come along. And while I was waiting for him, and contemplating the idea of waiting in general, I found that waiting could be so easily turned into a spiritual exercise. I came to see that I wasn't waiting for just this one person to come along and swim with me, but that I was waiting for something greater to happen. Exactly what I didn't know, but I got the opportunity to think about what or who it was that I was most deeply waiting for.

So I take it that you were ultimately waiting on a higher power — on God?

Yes, yes, it's so true! It became clearer that it was God whom I was waiting for. His presence was veiled in so many guises and situations.

Your words bring to mind a passage which I believe is in your book Psalm. *You have a copy there on your shelf. Let me read the passage to you.*

231

Go right ahead.

"It is you who tells me of the longed for being. Your voice calls me to the far off land. Where am I now? Living on a rock. What's above me? Black night sky. What is under me? Hard board bed. How did I get here? Can't remember. But I remember there was a moment of trust — a long, full moment of trust that passed, that existed between us…I made a choice, a long time ago. I don't remember what it was but since then I've been falling. I don't think I mean I'm falling to the ground. I hope I don't mean I'm falling into hell. I'm falling toward you. I've been falling toward you since then.[18]

Yes, yes…I made that choice a long time ago.

Do you have any regrets?

Not at all. And I'm still falling, still waiting.

How should we "wait on God"?

By being gentle and patient both with yourself and with others, no matter what comes along. In this way, waiting becomes a fulfilling, very meaningful experience.

It's interesting how when we wait for someone to join us, we're also "waiting on God" because He is naturally within us. So, in a way, God is shared when two people meet — a type of higher communion happens.

Yes, that's true. As you know, the Creator's presence is everywhere, and everyone holds the kingdom within themselves.

You know, it just came to me that since God is everywhere, we become the best that we can be simply by uniting with Him, since through Him all things were created in the first place. In God, we realize our maximum potential, "we flow," as you like to say. We ride the waves.

That's so right. I'm glad you thought of that. Truly, we are all God's children sharing in His divinity. He's always there for us.

But exactly how do we share, especially when so many faiths differ? Do you believe that all paths to salvation are valid?

Well, I think if you live gently, honourably, focusing on the cultivation of your heart, good things are sure to follow. And I have posted a note on the wall up there which might help to answer your question. It goes like this: "There are as many paths to salvation as there are people willing to be saved."

That sounds faintly like the Japanese Zen poet Ikkyu, who said, "Many winding roads and paths lead to the top of the mountain, but at the peak, we all gaze at the single bright moon."

Very good, yes, I've heard of that. I do appreciate the ecumenical and interfaith approach. We were meant to connect with each other, to take care of each other, to check up on each other. It's all about communication.

So the universe is really a "You" and an "I" verse.

(Laughter). Great! And I'd also stress that "verse" part too. We were meant to be a cosmic poem of harmony *in* harmony.

233

That's why Socrates said, "The part can't be well unless the whole is well."

And that could be why the ancient Indian philosopher Nagarjuna[19] said, "We're not independent, but interdependent." In essence, we are one body, and the whole body needs attention. Everything is intricately connected – you just have to let go and ride the flow to see things as they really are.

Praying the Dream True

I remember what you once said about attention: "Attention is holy – that's why everyone wants it."

That's true. Giving someone your one hundred per cent undivided attention is like extending a blessing. For lack of attention, people will rock the boat, and I mean really rock it!

So how do we steady it?

You might try praying. I think we've been called to "cultivate the field" through prayer. It all started in Eden. We're meant to be caretakers of every flower in the garden. And we're meant to be co-creators too. I think the Creator wants as many people as possible to share in His joy and charity. I say worry less, pray more!

You've said before that prayer may be equated with play. How so?

Well, since Jesus has been described as "Joy," then prayer should be a happy, unselfconscious way of participating in that Joy. Nothing should be excessively hard if you love what you are doing. Through love, and the joy and play of love, all things may become prayer.

Have you seen the power of prayer manifest itself in your life?

Yes, very often, it seems to me. I'm with St. John Chrysostom who said, "Prayer changes even the substance of things."

Once you told me that a relative's prayer helped to save your life. I think the incident happened back in the mid-eighties when you briefly returned to the USA. You were out by Merton's Monastery of Gethsemani in Kentucky.

Yes, it was about 3 a.m. and I was changing buses to get back to Olean. I don't know why this individual came after me, but he chased me out to the parking lot and threw me face down on the ground. He squeezed his forearm on my gullet and said, "You're gonna die – I'm gonna kill you!" At that point, I was able to suck up enough air to say, "Please, friend, don't do this to me. You really don't want to do this to me, do you?" But he seemed not to hear, and only squeezed tighter. I thought how sad it was to die in an empty, deserted place like this. And I thought that of all the people who were going to be shocked and disturbed by my death, it would be my niece

Connie because I had just visited her, and she had told me how careful I had to be on my trip back to Olean. Then there's this business about how, in the final moment, your whole life passes before your eyes. Well, it did, and as it was passing, I kept on hearing this old song, "It's three o'clock in the morning, it's three o'clock in the morning…"

It's really amazing how you remember everything so vividly.

(Laughter). Near-death experiences do that. But to go on. Suddenly, he relaxed his hold, stood up, went through my wallet, and then ran off. Later, when I spoke with my niece about the incident, I learned that Connie had been praying for me close to the time that it had happened…

The power of prayer.

Yes, most definitely.

What about the efficacy of prayers directed toward people that we don't even know? If I'm walking down the street and I see someone who may need help and I pray for that person, does that do any good?

Of course! It's good to send out wholesome, generative thoughts. The individual can affect the universal. But you might want to lend a hand, too. Helping people makes you feel better about everything, including yourself. I mean, giving food and drink to someone who's hungry or sharing a good book or paper can do a lot to create happiness. Just be sincere.

Yes, and I think the Letter of James states, "Faith, without works, is dead."[20] *But tell me, if I pray often, am I creating in and around myself a "positive energy field" so that when I walk through a hostile environment, my very presence might change it for the better?*

Sure, there's something to that.

Do you feel, then, that prayer is the most important thing to do in life?

I think so. And when you really come to believe this and start putting your conviction into practice, then praying yourself into the moment and into the work of the moment gets to be second nature. I think that prayer is a way of doing instantaneous good for all things in all places. It's a way of sending out love everywhere at once. It's a power that everyone has access to, and it can transfigure the world. Prayer makes everything you do more real, lasting, meaningful, and fruitful. Through prayer, everything just flowers and flows. It's a way of living and giving.

What if one can't pray?

Then go to some quiet, scenic place and rest. Listen to a bird's song. Take in the stillness. Or do something creative. Sing, dance, paint, smile. Help somebody. You know, feel the morning's presence in every leaf. Share your joy. I feel all of that counts as prayer, especially if it proceeds from a joyful, loving heart.

If we pray more often, might we better perceive how a tree reflects the glory of God?

Certainly. I think our good friend St. Francis would agree. We have the "Book of Scripture," but we also have the "Book of Nature." After all, the earth is God's great temple. You can say the stars are His candles, the mountains His altars, the flowers His incense...

If through contemplating nature one discovers higher truths that inspire one to lead a peaceful, meditative existence, is it necessary to read Scripture?

Both are important. Your question reminds me of Marcus Aurelius' *Meditations*. He was working with nature quite a bit, not any form of holy writing. And in his Stoic way, he came to so many of the same points of wisdom and good counsel that the Prophets spoke of.

And yet this same Roman emperor martyred many early Christians.

Yes, but we're human after all, imperfect, susceptible to errors brought on by misinformation and ignorance. We do make mistakes. We must forgive him. But when he wrote his *Meditations*, he knew what he was doing.

What is the relationship between forgiveness and prayer?

I think the two are inseparable. Forgiveness is a prime component of love. Forgiving someone who has offended you really puts your compassion to the test. Do you love enough to forgive? Do you forgive enough so that you might love more? Jesus said, "As we forgive, so shall we be forgiven." Now maybe this does not mean forgive and forget, but certainly forgive. Real forgiveness means that you just don't forgive and be done with it, but you also pray for those who have wronged you. We have every reason to be comfortable with forgiveness because we know that our Father in heaven is a God of forgiveness. We can trust Him, because in heaven's own time He will forgive each of us. I really do believe that.

Yes, we were talking about this some time ago when we were walking along "cat alley," as you refer to your outside walkway. Perhaps the amount of injustice done to us does test our capacity to forgive.

That's right.

And ours is not to question or judge or condemn the source of injustice; ours is only to forgive.

That's what Jesus tells us. There are no limitations to forgiveness because there are no limitations to love. Then there's that little thing about cleaning your own house out before you start advising someone else to clean theirs.

What about self-forgiveness?

Well, you really can't forgive your neighbour until you learn how to start forgiving yourself. In so many ways, your neighbour is yourself. If you can begin being gentle with yourself, pretty soon that gentleness will extend to everyone around you. When we forgive ourselves and each other, things that interfere with the flow of holiness dissolve. Real communion happens. Everything flows and flows.

But, then again, it's so common to focus the blame on someone or something else.

A lot of that happens because of how you may have been treated when you were a child. If you were roughly handled and abused, sure, forgiving will be harder. You won't be able to readily forgive your parents, yourself, your neighbours, or anyone else who may have done you harm. Exercising love in this situation will indeed be difficult. But how much easier it would be if we lived in a more forgiving world! I'm reminded of Max Beerbohm's story "The Happy Hypocrite."

How does it go?

A man named Lord George Hell, the worst of people, fell in love with a very good woman. In order to win her, he had to act like a very good man. So he feigned all kinds of good behaviour to attract her. But most importantly, throughout the whole charade, he wore a carefully contrived mask of innocence.

Was this an actual mask?

Yes, it was. Now, at a certain point in his attempts to woo her, one of Lord Hell's past lovers saw through his disguise, and in jealousy she sought to expose him. So at the moment he was winning the innocent maiden over, the angry woman suddenly stormed in and ripped off Hell's mask, only to discover that his face had transformed into that of an angel!

So the man was changed through imitating the good, even though he was not good to begin with. His assumed purity – however divisive – eventually made an impression on his very body.

Exactly. So if you already know that you're not the best of fellows, you can at least practise acting like one, and that's a first step. Through practice, you may catch on. Shakespeare said it's not always necessary for knowledge to precede experience. Your body may begin to understand before your mind does, especially if you immerse yourself in a routine.

And that can be a routine of forgiveness, a plan of peace and prayer, a determined, consistent effort to gently impart love, and to receive it.

Sure. Just as the earth has a rhythm, and the seasons do as well, so all of us, I think, profit in leading some sort of rhythmic existence that goes with the flow and keeps pace with the lovebeats of the heart. That's what everything ultimately reduces to – love is at the core of what really matters.

Love-Waves Always

Robert, what are your thoughts about the new millennium?

I just hope people go on living as best they can and peace gets more possible. I hope that there will be more forgiveness in the next one thousand years. That way life can go on.

What major changes do you see happening?

I think that we will steadily become more receptive to what love really means. There will be a collective understanding of where we came from, where we are, and where we are going. I feel that we will increasingly sense a greater interconnection and unity with the whole of existence, and so we will become more gentle, more intuitive, more caring, more giving, more loving as a result. As the love increasingly flows, I believe that we will tap into our dreams more, and, by doing that, make better sense of our lives because the unconscious and conscious states will be wonderfully linked through a palpable, transfiguring love. The cosmos was born in joyful love, and toward joyful love we are heading.

Do you think that art, science, spirituality, and all fields will remain specialized or do you see a great synthesis taking shape?

I sense that art, science, and spirituality are going to start merging beautifully. But for those with limited vision, who want to keep religion out of human progress, I fear they will be increasingly left out of the syncretistic nature of the times. I really don't know anybody who would say otherwise. Now maybe I just hang out with the wrong crowd, but if you tune in to the BBC, for instance, you know that a "unified field theory" is truly taking place. Almost anybody who thinks about science, nature, and the environment has got to start thinking about how the cosmos was put together. This is where religion may help, not hinder. And the theologians would benefit by listening to the scientists – that's already happening, anyway. So I'm genuinely optimistic about the whole thing. Millions and millions of people are realizing that the world is one world, and are acting in ways that support this reality. We really are related to each other – we are parts of each other, a big family, and that's why we should try to help one another. It's one spaceship, as they say. I think that we are moving toward a more unified, loving universe as we journey to the stars.

What do you think about the role of women in the next millennium?

As women get increasingly involved in the affairs of the world, I have a strong feeling that they will greatly contribute to international peace. They will help bring things up-to-date in a way that truly makes sense because they will be gentle in what they do. Men tend to fix things in ways that intimidate, or frighten, but women, because they are nurturing and family-oriented, have a good idea how things should fit together. One might say that the last millennium has been overwhelmingly masculine in nature. I think that in the next one thousand years, society will increasingly embrace the feminine so that everything may come to a balance.

Lately there seems to be more emphasis on the nature of God being feminine. What do you think of this?

God is beyond masculine and feminine distinction, and all saints and well-rounded theologians understand this. But I think that people are psychologically oriented to seeing the nature of the Creator as being masculine or feminine.

Now, at last, it's time for confession. You know, Robert, I'm getting older.

So what? I'm hitting ninety, as you say.

(Laughter). No, really, we all are getting older, and as we mature, we begin to realize that we just don't know everything and inevitably never will.

Socrates said the same.

Right, but what I'm asking is, how much should we know? How do we live so that when we die, we don't feel like we're still desperately searching?

I think that at the beginning of the quest, it's natural to throw yourself into the whole thing and try to get as far as you can, oftentimes without seeking heaven's help. But then you begin to realize that life isn't a high jump, something you must accomplish once and for all. Every day we go a little further. Sometimes all we can do is tie our shoelaces, which is an art in itself. Gradually we come to see how it's not about squeezing everything we can into life. It's about doing our own little part well, as long as we don't become insensitive to others trying to do their parts.

So like St. Paul states, "Love does not insist on its own way."[21]

That's right. Pushing tends to create imbalance and upsets the flow. Living isn't a "one-man show." Being alive means you are alive with many other things, all of which are heaven-born and divinely nurtured. That's why prayer and heaven's help get to be increasingly important. Time, if nothing else, teaches us this, and as it does, any frustration we may feel transforms into hope. We at last give ourselves to the flow because we have learned to trust in its rhythm and source. Some of us find out about this sooner rather than later, but, in the end, the waters lead to the same place, to a new beginning, to the infinite powers and possibilities of love. Yes, old boy, the important thing is to love – *just love, love, love!* Keep on loving everybody and everything, as much as you can. Take this love everywhere you go, and with it you can help everything to grow.

So love-waves always?

Yes, love waves all ways!

(Laughter). I see, and I'm trying to see even better. We have such a short time to figure everything out.

That's where you're wrong. Life isn't a problem box – it's a joy! You just have to savour it, little by little. You'll see; you'll find your way. And you don't have to go too far. When people think that the quest for an infinite God is eternal, they begin to fear that they will never have enough time, whether in this life or the next, to know

Him. But God is in your heart as well, a place where time does not exist. He transcends us, yet He dwells within us. I'm thinking of a Sufi proverb that goes, "If you walk toward Him, He comes running."

Knock, and it shall be opened.

Precisely. And when the door is opened, the whole room gets filled with light.

You know, after all this spiritual dialogue, I'm left wondering about a phrase I've heard many say. What is "common wisdom"?

I think it's when you learn from what's around you. Nature is a good teacher. There's so much there to study and absorb. If you watch the waves and listen to them, you're sure to learn something.

Perhaps that's why St. Paul states, "Ever since the creation of the world, God's glory abounds in the things that have been made."[22] Now all at once I remember that walk we took some years ago on the far end of the isle. You asked me to look into the water and tell you what I saw.

What did you see?

The sky, the mountains, and ourselves reflected in it. I interpreted this to be how all things are like one moving body, flowing, rippling, coursing like a dream. There were other things too, but what comes to mind is how much I felt myself to be a part of nature.

Yes, all things are a part of nature. People too. The fisherman and the farmer can teach. In many ways, they're saying the same thing you might learn at a higher institution, but rather than use a blackboard or book, they instruct through their work, through their very lives. Stop a moment and see how a farmer tends his crops. Take a look at a fisherman mending his net. Watch how the ships sail. Look at how the wind blows, how the birds move with it across the sky. This is common wisdom, what esoteric wisdom ultimately points to. It's the kind of thing you might find in your own backyard, that quiet place where once upon a time, a seed became a garden. But if people have to go to the world's end to become enlightened, then let them go, I say. It's good to ride the free wave.

Robert, before we close, is there anything else you'd like to say? Is there any more wisdom you'd like to impart?

Now is that what I've been doing all this time – giving you wisdom? Old folks like me just want to unload. (Laughter). Well, for the record, and I can't say it enough, try to live as purely and as simply and as gently as you can. Relax. Be flexible. Be forgiving. Be creative. Be loving. You are a peacemaker. Those who cross your path may need you, as you may need them. Remember all things under heaven have their special relationship with God. Listen, be discerning, use all the radar you can generate in your waking moments and in your dreams, but don't judge – let God do that. Just try to keep the balance, because you're in it for the long run. We all are.

But can you see where the path might take me? What can I expect?

You'll find out. Just take your time. No matter what happens, go slow, and keep on going. Respect what comes your way. Trust in the flow. We were made to go forward; we were built like that. So watch every step. Keep focused, stay fit, and keep your intentions pure. Don't drop everything if something beautiful or sad happens. Exercise sight and insight. If you get distracted you may lose the path, and without a path, there can be no prize.

And if I do trip up?

Get back on beam as fast as you can. Whole world's watching, counting on you to do the right thing, the loving thing. So let in the light whenever, wherever you can. And after cultivating the glow for a while, let it go, let it flow, transmit it, and you're sure to receive more along the way.

That sounds great, but it's also a lot of homework.

Heartwork and artwork take a whole lifetime, my boy. But you know that for a flower to bloom, it must first inch its way through the dark. And a flower owes its beauty to its roots, which remain forever hidden. Just keep at it. Raise the sparks! Incense without fire is useless; in order for a bell to ring, it must be struck.

No shortcuts?

You don't need any – none of us do. It's all about rhythm. So make a plan. Visualize. Actualize. Get the flow going, and stick to the beat. It gets easier after that.

Sounds like jazz.

You bet. But this kind of jazz – in a way like the jazz of Duke Ellington – is about saving the planet, about leaving the world a better place than we found it. And everybody has their own special solo to play.

So we better get hoppin'?

Amen to that.

One last thing – I'd like to read to you something Thomas Merton wrote which summarizes a lot of what we've been talking about.

Please do, Steve.

"At the center of our being is a point of nothingness which is untouched by sin and illusion, a point of pure truth, a point or spark which belongs entirely to God, which is never at our disposal, from which God disposes of our lives, which is inaccessible to the fantasies of our mind or the brutalities of our will. This little point of nothingness and of absolute poverty is the pure glory of God in us. It is, so to speak, His name written in us, as our poverty, as our indigence, as our dependence, as our sonship. It is like a pure diamond, blazing with the invisible light of heaven. It is in everybody, and if we could see it we would see these billions of points of light coming together in the face

and blaze of a sun that would make all the darkness and cruelty of life vanish completely…I have no problem for this seeing. It is only given. But the gate of heaven is everywhere."[23]

Excellent. Beautiful and true. Right up there with the best things that have been written about heaven, truth, and the Spirit. Thank you so very much. You've given me joy, more than you know. Your coming here has been a blessing. This is going to be a great day. Everything begins today.

¹ *Concrete Poetry: An International Anthology.* Edited by Stephen Bann. London: Magazine Editions, 1975, 194–195.

² In Buddhist terminology, a *Bodhisattva* is a person who is worthy of the paradise of Nirvana, but elects not to partake of that bliss; instead, he helps others attain Nirvana as well. In essence, no one is free until all are free.

³ The Desert Fathers were early Christian ascetics who occupied the wastelands of Egypt and the Near East during the first millennium of Christianity. For more on the topic, see Helen Waddell's *The Desert Fathers,* Ann Arbor: University of Michigan Press, 1957 and Derwas Chitty's *The Desert A City,* New York: St. Vladimir's Seminary Press, 1966. Merton also wrote a book on the topic: *The Wisdom of the Desert.* New York: New Directions, 1960.

⁴ Mircea Eliade (1907–1986) was a historian and philosopher of comparative religion and metaphysics. Born in Romania, he studied at the University of Calcutta and was especially versed in Indian philosophy. He held professorships at Calcutta, Bucharest, the Sorbonne and Chicago University and wrote many books and papers on the systematic study of world religions such as *The Sacred and the Profane* (1957) and *Myths, Dreams, and Mysteries* (1960). He is perhaps best remembered for his monumental editing of *The Encyclopedia of Religion,* MacMillan Publishing, 1987.

⁵ Proverbs 23.17.

⁶ The artists Ulf T. Knaus of Salzburg, Vito Lo Greco of Rome, and Niko Eliou of Patmos were good friends of Lax and have routinely exhibited their work on Patmos. Lax regularly attended their exhibitions. Of note is that all three artists, including the Belgian Olivier de Kerchove, greatly assisted Lax in the stages of his return to Olean, New York, in the summer of 2000.

⁷ See *The ABC's of Robert Lax* (Edited by D. Miller and N. Zurbrugg. London: Stride, 1999) for references to Lax's saintly nature. See also *The Merton Seasonal,* vol. 26, No. 1, Spring 2001.

[8] *Microbe Man* refers to an Athenian who had recently visited the area where Lax lived and took offense to Lax's many cats, exclaiming that they were spreading disease; as a result, the cats were taken away by island authorities for a short while.

[9] The Jesuit father Teilhard de Chardin (1881–1955) was influenced by the lives and teachings of the Christian mystics since his youth. At the same time, he expressed an early and intense interest in geology and paleontology. His life's work came to be dedicated to integrating the fields of science and spirituality and reconciling scientific and religious truths. Deeply influenced by the process of evolution, Teilhard saw the great outpouring of creation as centred in the "Cosmic Christ." His best-known books include *The Phenomenon of Man, Hymns of the Universe,* and his autobiography, *The Heart of the Matter.*

[10] Seraphim of Sarov (1756–1833) remains one of Orthodox Russia's best-loved saints. He taught that the primary aim of life is to acquire the Holy Spirit through *theosis* (deification, becoming like God through His superabundant grace); in doing so, one comes to radiate divine love. A great lover of animals and nature, he may be compared to St. Francis of Assisi.

[11] *Ahimsa,* a Buddhist term for non-violence and love for all things that exist, comparable to the Christian *agape.*

[12] Amphilochius Makris (1889–1970) remains an exceedingly popular holy man of Patmos. Numerous miracles and psychic phenomena have been attributed to the monk. See *Elder Amphilochius Makris: A Contemporary Personality of Patmos.* Archimandrite Paul Nikitaras. Monastery of St. John Publications, Patmos, 1990.

[13] The Monastery of the Annunciation is located near the medieval Monastery of St. John. The picturesque, fortress-like structure occupies a site where stood a small church dedicated to the Annunciation of Mary (the Evangelismos). However in 1937, the monk Amphilochius Makris of Patmos founded the Convent of the Annunciation (Evangelismos) on the same site. There he served as the nuns' spiritual advisor. His cell and relics are venerated in a special chapel there.

[14] *The Philokalia* ("The Way of the Good") is a multi-volume spiritual classic written in Greek between the fourth and fifteenth centuries by masters of the Eastern Orthodox tradition. Compiled in the eighteenth century, it has greatly influenced the Eastern Church. *The Way of the Pilgrim* was first published in 1884 and chronicles an anonymous Orthodox pilgrim's journey through nineteenth century Russia and Siberia. The book emphasizes the need to "pray without ceasing." *The Ladder of Divine Ascent,* by St. John Climacus (579–649 AD), was a foundational handbook pertaining to the ascetic life of Eastern Orthodox monasticism, and remains so to this day. *The Monk of Mt. Athos,* by Archimandrite Sophrony (translated by Rosemary Edwards, St. Vladimir's Seminary Press, New York, 1973), relates to the struggles of the monk Silouan, who became a leading spiritual director on Mt. Athos in the early twentieth century. His philosophy is much akin to the thought expressed by the Desert Fathers and Hesychasts, who favoured humility, silence, and heart-centred thought and prayer.

[15] Hebrews 13.1-2.

[16] Genesis 18.10-12.

[17] James Harford, who met Lax in 1952, is Executive Director Emeritus, American Institute of Aeronautics and Astronautics. He is writing a book about the Lax, Merton and Rice friendship.

[18] Robert Lax. *Psalm.* Zurich: Pendo-Verlag, 1991, 20, 24.

[19] Nagarjuna lived during the second/third century. He was one of the premier philosophers of Buddhism and was the principal founder of the Madhyamika School, which emphasizes the emptiness of matter and the illusory nature of all appearances. One of Nagarjuna's primary teachings relates how all things derive their being and nature through mutual interdependence and are nothing (empty) in themselves.

[20] James 2.12.

[21] 1 Corinthians 13.5.

[22] Romans 1.20.

[23] Thomas Merton. *Conjectures Of A Guilty Bystander.* New York: Doubleday, 1968, 158.

EPILOGUE

Beginner's Mind

During my last meeting with Robert, the old poet rose from his chair and walked to the window of his hermitage, which overlooked the Bay of Skala. He surveyed the water and sky and in a slow, meditative voice said, "There's a big white bird wheeling over the waves." It seemed as though he were reflecting aloud, and I did not give much thought to his words until a few hours later, after I had said my final farewell and was heading down to the sea.

It was late afternoon. My descent had been a melancholy one because I had been contemplating if I would ever see Lax again. Every so often I fingered a small silver cross that I had asked him to bless, and the memory of Robert taking it into his hands and shutting his eyes in prayer did give me some sense of comfort.

As I made my way through the winding streets I eventually came to a clearing that allowed for a direct view to the harbour. Suddenly a large gull appeared, circling in the sky. Immediately I thought of my teacher's words, and as I did so, a strong gust arose. This in itself was not unusual, since Patmos tends to be a windy isle, but it was what the wind had stirred that took hold of my attention.

Earlier that day, I had brought Lax two large handfuls of bougainvillea petals that I had collected near the shore. They were meant to be a goodbye gift, and it was my intent to shower his home with them, but after thanking me for the petals, he asked that I gently place them out on the porch. Now, these very same petals, which had blown down to the lower levels of Kastelli, were swirling about me, spinning with each gust of wind. At once I took this to be a sign that Robert would always be with me, that he would always be "around and around," as both the whirling petals and the wheeling bird seemed to testify. Moreover, my "flower gift" had come back in the form of a reciprocal blessing, as though Robert had returned the favour. And as I thought of these mystical events, the bells in the nearby church of St. Prokopi began to ring out the hour. In a heartbeat I remembered what Lax had said earlier: *In order for a bell to ring, it must be struck.*

This was the moment of my sounding, so to speak. My consciousness had been struck with three consecutive omens – a bird, the bougainvillea petals, and the church bells, and each of these things intoned that an awakening of some sort was in effect. I thought of going back to speak with Robert about it, but quickly decided against it. My intuition suggested that somehow Lax knew what had taken place.

Deeply moved by this incident, I gathered up a number of the flower petals and continued my descent to Skala. Oblivious to the activity of the port town, I walked out to the lengthy pier facing the sea and began to reflect on how Robert had influenced me, both in the past few months and over the years.

Certainly our meetings and conversations had gone well. Since 1993, his insight and counsel had always enlightened and inspired me. But more than anything else, I think it was his presence which consistently impressed me, the way he moved and spoke, the whole manner of his peaceful, happy being. Calmly, and with subtle power, he intoned that anything is possible in God, providing one is compassionate and attentive. And coming from a voice like his, that meant a great deal. Lax's life in itself had proved that a man could love so much that he became a living blessing. He gracefully showed how creature, creation, and Creator could harmoniously merge and give birth to radiant possibilities. He revealed bright paths of fulfillment and freedom. There was no "growing old" in Lax, only the joy of new beginnings, and I think it was that kind of unique inspiration, that kind of confident charge that I had been searching for all of my adult life.

To be sure, my meetings with Lax had been spiritual encounters – there is no other way to describe them. I experienced a type of communion with him, certainly not in an ecclesiastical fashion, but in a cosmically creative way, almost as if I had entered a forest or climbed a mountain and communed with the sanctity of nature. Lax seemed to be a microcosm of the beauty surrounding him, and I often wondered if his open, highly receptive being had allowed for the holy rhythms of Patmos to enter and play within his soul. When he spoke, he orchestrated his expressions according to the changes in the environment around him, so that one word, said in concert with a vibrant colour created by a sunset, could impart so much more than ordinary speech. In his quiet, poetic resonance, he reminded me of an Eastern sage, the "True Man" of Chuang Tzu, the "Man of Te" who in motion is like water; at rest, like a mirror; in response, like an echo; who in his stillness, remains pure. Lax naturally possessed what the Asian mystics term "Beginner's Mind," wherein all things are possible, and, like Patmos itself, his presence was a place to start from, to be reborn and begin a revitalized understanding of the world.

The humble poet was truly a springboard to a higher reality, to the power of the sacred in everyday life. The apprehension of this divine "flow" seemed very real and palpable in his presence. When he entered a room, dimensions to peace and ways to enlightenment opened because his affirming demeanour always pointed to something greater operating in the universe. For those who experienced this liberating energy, these sensations might continue hours after exchanging greetings with the sage. I remember how after spending long evenings with Lax, I would leave his hermitage and feel as though I had landed on earth for the first time. Everything was new, happy, beautiful; everywhere I found serenity, centrality, and light. Indeed, after pausing outside his dwelling to quickly write down the highlights of our exchanges – even the interpretations of the many silences we had shared – I would descend into Skala blessed and seeking to bless, undisturbed by the pressing crowds of tourists and the loud sounds of the waterfront. Like a man in a dream I would go out to the massive concrete pier where Robert and I did our walking and there recline by the waters, my eyes turned to the stars.

I remember the twinkling, glowing lights. With them I pulsated as though I were exploding into infinite realms, and all the while I was laughing, beaming, radiating because it felt so good to be lying on the wave-flecked dock with my head spinning in the clouds.

Yet my ecstasy did not lead to oblivion. Lax typically gave me scraps to feed any "creature cousin" I might encounter en route to Skala, so I would happily toss the food into the sea and watch the marine life consume the remains of our dinner, which, at rare times, could be fish.

It was interesting how the fish had come from the sea, and into the sea their remnants had returned. Things therefore seemed cyclic on Patmos, and this was particularly true in a spiritual sense, for here, ultimately everything began and ended with prayer. As Lax had expressed:

> Everything that exists
> can turn to prayer;
> even the water,
> even the air.

from Robert Lax,
"A Song For Our Lady"

Flying Fish

Sitting by the waterside, I remembered the many seaside walks and talks that we had engaged in over the years. Every evening, Robert would descend from his hermitage and meet me outside the Apollon Travel Agency or at the adjoining Arion café, both of which faced the sea. He came by at about 6 or 6:30 p.m., beaming his beautiful "I love you" smile. Lax almost always wore sunglasses, a hat of some sort (usually a Greek fisherman's hat), and carried a canvas grocery bag and a sizable walking staff. As for his manner of dress, it typically fell into four "styles," although Robert would never think that he had any conscious style at all. But he seemed to have a "Greek Fisherman" look when he wore his bright blue jeans and Levi's jacket. And when he wore his tweed coat and baggy black pants, he looked a bit like an eccentric college professor. And when he donned his worn white trousers and jacket, I referred to him as the "Circus Sage." But his most interesting (and sadly infrequent) mode of dress, I felt, was the "Taoist hermit" look, which included a long, wide-sleeved coat and an oversized straw hat with dangling tassel-cords. Again, I don't believe Robert dressed to create any special effect. His clothes were typically rough-cut to begin with. But it was interesting how his attire — most of which was given him, owing to his dependence on divine Grace — seemed congruent with various aspects of his personality.

So we would meet in the evening and Lax would say something like, "I feel a plan coming on, but I'd like to know what you think," or "What's your plan? What do you think we should do?" In any event, after deciding how we would spend our time together, we would always begin with a walk along the sea which took about 45 minutes to an hour. Afterward, we would pay a visit to the grocer Panteli, one of Robert's close friends, and talk at length. Once in a while we visited the homes of islanders Lax knew to be sick. We also bought supplies of various sorts such as yogurt, vegetables, olive oil, grape juice, small cakes, jam, and especially fish for his many cats. Visiting the fish market was always fun because the fishing folk would hang around and swap stories with "Kalos Petros" (Good Peter), as they sometimes called Lax. And they would joke that Lax spent more money on his cats than on himself.

After the shopping was done we would slowly ascend the hill of Kasteli leading up to his home. Usually I carried the fish bags because they were the heaviest, and Lax took the remaining groceries.

Those evening ascents were quiet, meditative, full of deep listening, keen sensing. The dying sun, the living moon, the whitewashed homes and the food we carried up all seemed to meld together into a holy wine, an earthy, blessed vintage which we drank step by step. On arrival, I would proceed to cut the fish for the cats and feed them, while Lax supervised. Then we got our own meal ready, which always took time, because Robert, in his natural Zen-like manner, performed every action – be it operating a blender or turning on a stove – with the whole of his being. Chopping vegetables was a meditative act in itself, and even pouring a glass of bottled water, which we regularly drank, seemed to take on sacramental overtones. Therefore to eat comfortably with Lax, dedication and patience were required, as was the saying of Grace, which might proceed from Scripture or, in a more creative fashion, could take the form of a poem.

When the meal had finished, pound cake topped with marmalade jam was the typical desert. Sometimes Lax would treat me to Swiss chocolate, for which he seemed to have a fondness. Then, after clearing the table and washing the dishes, we would talk about what the day had meant to us. He might read his latest poems to me, or would show me recent sketches and "zip-zap swirls." Or he would open a book, even the dictionary, and discuss a word or passage and then ask me to make copies of similar meaningful passages and distribute them to visiting artists who were working on the isle.

Sometimes we simply sat in silence and listened to the wind. We might also reflect on our walk along the harbour and discuss things that we had felt as we were walking. On some nights there would be a knock at the door, and a friend of Lax might come in, and we would talk and joke together. Periodically I would tell Lax that like Aristotle, he had his own "peripatetic school" or walking institute of higher education. Lax would reply that the "walking-learning connection" went back to Genesis, when Adam and Eve walked in paradise with the Lord and received wisdom.

Those seaside walks were always special. The honey-gold evening light bathed everything in a holy glow. Thus illuminated, Lax and I would carefully cross the promenade, always keeping an eye out for wayward motorcycles. After reaching the lengthy concrete pier, we settled down into an easy, free-flowing rhythm, a rolling gait like two boats gently adrift on the waves. We took slow, contemplative steps, exchanging feelings with and without words because we mainly communicated through our cadence, movements, and expressions. Sometimes Lax would point to something and make a comment that was meant to invite discussion, or I might do the same. At times he giggled and in a childlike way whispered, "Good...good...," almost purring the words like a cat, and that would move me to laugh, and then we ended up walking and laughing as though mildly inebriated.

On some evenings visiting friends and artists would join us and partake in our discussions. Locals too would come by and chat. If they had considerable news to relate, they might walk with us up and down the pier, intermittently pausing when making dramatic points of emphasis. And when the fishing boats docked, particularly those from Kalymnos, it was not unusual for the fishermen to loudly hail Robert with a hearty *"Kirios Petros!"* (Sir Peter!), and then come over and embrace him, all the while remarking what a good and holy man he was.

Afterwards, when it got quiet, Lax and I might stroll over to the net menders and idly reflect on the metaphysics of their art, or we might sit for a while and study the rippling shadows of the swaying trees or gaze out over the sea. Once a flying fish leaped out of the water, surprising us both. "Did you see that?" Lax had asked. "Now that doesn't happen too often!"

In this manner we passed the time. All the while the boats would go sailing in and out, and the birds would wheel overhead, and the sky would turn red-gold and then pink-purple as the sun descended and the shadows lengthened.

If we did not sit, we might instead lean over a chest-high metal railing. Lax would then say, "What a great bar – real nice." Playing along, I would ask, "What'll ya have?" And he would answer, "Gimme that secret drink again." "You mean the mystic brew, Captain Robo?" "That's it!" he would affirm. "That's what I'd like to have – and I think you should have one with me." And together we'd drink in the whole lazy evening, saying nothing more because everything was already speaking, and we were happy just listening.

As night fell, the time would come for us to go. We usually left together, although every once in a while Lax would say, "I think I'm going to go up now – it'll be a solo ascent this time. We'll see each other tomorrow; in the meantime, don't forget to take care of Steve for me." And almost in a shy way he would turn to leave, and I would watch him move on until he disappeared from sight altogether. Then, when I could not hear his staff hitting the pavement any longer, I too would turn to go my way.

Bringing Things to Bear

As I sat by the sea and reminisced, I began to understand why Robert had periodically left me to myself. I think he was trying to gently convey what every teacher must impart to their students – the journey to self- discovery and spiritual fulfillment is, in many ways, a solitary one. "While the master may open the door," as the early Taoists remarked, "the disciple must enter by himself." It may be said that the entire student–teacher relationship hints of this impending farewell, when the disciple, having been inspired and equipped by the master, embarks upon the next stage of his spiritual journey.

Through his life and art, Lax had quietly empowered me with the conviction that it was indeed possible to lead a creative, loving life and bear fruit for oneself and others. We had been called to work and play in the same beautiful garden. As Scripture testifies, "We have been raised from the dead in order that we might bear fruit for God" (Romans 7.4). In bringing things to bear, Lax had taught that this entire process is dependent on love born through communication. It always remains a two-way street. When he spoke about my college teaching and university life in general, he would tell me, "Your students need you, just as you need them."

This emphasis on interdependence was highlighted one evening when we entered an incense-filled chapel in

Skala and lit candles together. First, Lax obtained his flame from one of the many candles already burning in a golden sandbox. In turn, I received my light from Lax's candle. "Do you see?" he said, motioning to the many flames. "One candle isn't enough – we all need each other if real light is to shine. We wouldn't be here if we didn't need each other. We're like little lights turning on in the world, guiding each other home." As I looked into the fire, it came to me how a glow almost identical to it had radiated in Lax's dwelling on the first night that I had met him.

In many ways, Patmos was the holy site where I came to be spiritually "born again." This is where I had come to fruition. The isle had become for me a sacred school of love, a place to cultivate inner wisdom and compassion so that with *agape* I might re-enter a world desperately in need of harmony. And years ago, there seemed to be mystical indications that this transformation of the heart would come to pass.

When I was about 25, a priest whom I had known suddenly died, and shortly thereafter, he came to me in a dream. He spoke from the tower of a castle and said, "*When you paint God, use the fullness of your brush,*" an injunction which may have meant to literally take up icon work, which, in fact, I later began, partly through Lax's prompting. Allegorically speaking, the command could also have referred to the necessity for inner development – we are all "icons of God," and we paint our image according to how we live and love.

When I first came to Patmos in 1993 and saw the medieval Monastery of St. John with its high walls and towers, I immediately remembered the dream. I told Lax about it shortly after meeting him, and the blue-eyed Dreamcatcher smiled, and in poem form wrote it into his notebook, titling the verse "Steve's Dream," in this way artfully "catching it." And over the course of time, the dream steadily clarified and came true.

Through Lax's influence, I came to realize that "painting God" was exactly what I had all along been doing with my life – ultimately what anybody does with their life, whether in times of light or darkness – and Lax had helped me to discover the full range of my brush. Indeed, had I not met the sage-poet, my creative and academic evolution may never have significantly evolved. Authentic living therefore consisted of looking within and discovering one's gifts (particularly through the aid of a teacher), and as Lax had put it, "giving them back to the Giver in an unassuming, happy, and loving manner." Small wonder why Robert gave me one of his canvas grocery bags when I left him and hinted with a smile, "Maybe you'll fill it up with something."

Yet why had all this happened to me? Why had I met Lax in the first place? Perhaps it was because I had first come to Patmos broken in spirit. I had nearly lost faith in love, in the possibility of finding lasting joy in life, and put myself at the mercy of God. I had known Patmos to be a spiritual isle, a place of hope, miracles and revelation, and something told me that if I journeyed here, if I made the effort, I might save myself, or, better put, allow God to save me. And the waters were kind because they brought me to a tranquil site referred to in early Christianity as the "Isle of Love," owing to its relationship with St. John the Apostle, "the disciple whom Jesus most loved" (John 13.23).

In essence, I had "gone with the flow." I had "ridden the waves" to Patmos and had realized my dream through her beloved poet and peacemaker. And returning here again and again in a rhythmic way – almost with the consistency of a pulse or heartbeat – has helped me to cultivate and expand that vision. For over the years, my spirited treks to the sacred isle and happy communion with Robert have most abundantly and tangibly revealed to me the creative holiness of love. Indeed, my first letter to Lax, which I had enclosed in a small icon and had given him shortly before my boat left Patmos in 1993, succinctly reveals what the graced hermit meant to me from the beginning.

Petros:

Thank you so much for the talks, the walks, but most of all for the turns and pauses and the unsaid somethings and the shining of the light. Now the way is a little easier for me, and I'll be heading out to sea with a bit more paint on my brush (*Steve's Dream...*). I'll write to you every so often, but most of all, I'll read and walk with your work and remember you and grow...

You know, in a way, you've helped me not so much by human doing, but through human being. Sort of like how you looked at a fishing boat or gazed out over the waters. Things happened quietly between us, and I'd like to think they're still happening. *They are.* Already I see myself on Ocean Beach in San Francisco thinking of a special fisherman who came into my life at the right time.

God be with you, Petros! Thanks once more for sharing the invisible (yet still visible) gifts. I sense we shall see each other again someday, and I look forward to that meeting.

TAKE CARE,
STEVE

Soundings

At 11 p.m., about seven hours after what would be my final meeting with Lax, I boarded a ship bound for Piraeus, the port city near Athens. Ever since coming to Patmos, I had watched the ferries arrive and depart, and now it was my turn to go.

Lax had told me that when the ferry sounded its goodbye blast, he would beam me a "farewell flashlight signal" from his window. Though I knew that his hermitage was too distant for me to see his light, it did not matter. I still looked toward the mountain of Kastelli and waved because I saw Robert through the eye of my heart, and he, the same.

The ferry pulled away from the island and glided across the moonlit waters. Everything seemed dreamlike, surreal, as though my time on Patmos had been born of myth. In the white lunar glow I remembered what Lax had asked me just before I left him: "Do you have everything you need?"

"Yes, my teacher," I whispered, once more voicing my reply as I leaned over the wet, salty stern and stared into the deep. "And nothing will be lost," I quietly added, "but shared with many."

A cool brisk wind arose and gathered in intensity. The ship's frothy wake blew far and wide, and her creaking hull trembled in meeting the open sea. Those who had been lounging on deck now went below, but I remained outside and continued thinking of the man who long ago had opened his radiant soul and given me every good thing. What was he contemplating? I wondered. What dream-song, what prayer-poem played within him as my ship plied the Aegean?

I looked to the horizon and saw Patmos slip away into the night. Within minutes, the isle had become a little point of light, a star in the darkness, a bright spark planted in the nocturnal depths of creation. Echoing a phrase from Merton, it had once more become a "seed of contemplation" for all who would undertake the journey.

* * *

When I returned to San Francisco, one of the first things I did was walk out to Ocean Beach, where I often stroll and meditate. However, this time I came to pour a small ampoule of Patmian sea water into the Pacific. In this way, a little bit of Patmos would always be close to me, and something of a "shore-to-shore connection" between Robert and myself would be physically and metaphysically established.

Some weeks after I came back, and while thinking about my many meetings with Petros, I saw a dolphin leap out of the sea. I came closer to the water and noticed that a few roses had washed ashore. When I knelt to lift them out of the water, I found a brass bell.

*All the great lessons
have already been intoned;
but each generation
in its own holy freedom
must hear them differently.*

POSTSCRIPT

By late Spring of 2000, Robert Lax's health was rapidly failing. Through the help and support of Marcia and Jack Kelly and the assistance of Connie Brothers, he was encouraged to return to Olean, New York, the town of his birth. After a long and difficult journey by land and sea (Lax had never liked to fly), he at last returned to Olean on July 29 accompanied by family members and devoted friends. In this way, Robert literally made a "full circle" – his life of love had indeed become "a sphere encompassing beginnings and endings, beginning and end" (*Circus of the Sun*). Living true to his own voice and spirit, he had "traced out a sphere of love in the void."

A few months before Lax's arduous transit to the States, Robert appeared to me in a memorable dream. He was about to move to a new home and was giving away his possessions. Eventually he turned to me and asked, "What do you want?" Rather boldly I replied, "Your house." He smiled and said, "You know you can't have that." Then I asked him, "What can I have?" And he bent down and kissed the small gold cross around my neck. In essence,

Lax had demonstrated that the greatest gift was already within my possession, this being the Presence and Love of the Almighty – the "treasure within" which does not grow old or frail. It is this interior treasure which lies hidden in our souls, awaiting discovery. Thus Thomas Merton wrote, "Our real journey in life is interior; it is a matter of growth, deepening, and of an ever greater surrender to the creative love and grace in our hearts" (*Circular Letter to Friends*, September 1968).

Shortly after his arrival in Olean, Robert died peacefully in his sleep on September 26, 2000, the feast day of St. John the Divine, author of the Fourth Gospel and the Revelation, according to the Eastern Orthodox Church. His hilltop grave, situated near the friars he had known in his youth, overlooks the campus of St. Bonaventure University. Gently, quietly, the Dreamcatcher dreams anew.

Whatever is real in the world continues working…

The worker may go, but the work continues.

Robert Lax,
from *Homage to Wittgenstein*

turn
jun
gle

to
gar
den

with
out

des
troy
ing

a
sin
gle

flow
er

Robert Lax

REFLECTIONS ALONG THE WAY

Always remember that a great wind is bearing us across the sky.

—Ojibwa saying

God is Love... Love grants prophecies, miracles. Love is an abyss of illumination, a fountain of fire bubbling up to inflame the thirsty soul. It is the condition of angels, and the progress of eternity.

—St. John Climacus, from *The Ladder of Divine Ascent*

Dedicate your whole heart, your whole life to loving the Lord; blend your soul with His, and lose yourself in the sea of sweet love.

—Shri Jiva

Seek the trunk of the tree, and do not worry if the branches do or do not exist.

—Farid Al-Din Attar, from *The Conference of the Birds*

We are never wholly illuminated until we drink the wine of Love; we cannot know ourselves until we meet a master.

—Yunus Emre

As the soul gives life to the body,
So the sage gives life to the world.

—Hasidic saying

The sunlight is one and the same wherever it falls, but only bright surfaces like water, mirrors, and polished metal can reflect it fully. So is the divine light; it falls equally and impartially on all hearts, but only the pure and clean hearts of the good can reflect it.

—Shri Ramakrishna

What is a saint? A saint is someone who has achieved a remote human possibility. It is impossible to say what that possibility is. I think it has something to do with the energy of love. Contact with this energy results in the exercise of a kind of balance in the chaos of existence. A saint does not dissolve the chaos; if he did, the world would have changed long ago. I do not think that a saint dissolves the chaos even for himself, for there is something arrogant and warlike in the notion of a man setting the universe in order.

It is a kind of balance that is the saint's glory. He rides the drifts like an escaped ski. His course is the caress of the hill. His track is a drawing of the snow in a moment of its particular arrangement with wind and rock. Something in him so loves the world that he gives himself to the laws of gravity and chance. Far from flying with the angels, he traces with the fidelity of a seismograph needle the state of the solid bloody landscape. His house is dangerous and finite, but he is at home in the world. He can love the shape of human beings, the fine and twisted shapes of the heart. It is good to have among us such men, such balancing monsters of love.

—Leonard Cohen, *Beautiful Losers*

a saint
a saint
a saint

was on
his way
to heaven

when his
favorite
theologian
came and
told him
it was
wrong

the saint
then felt
as I do
when you
tell me
it is
wrong

when you
tell me
it is
wrong
for me
to love
you

Robert Lax.
Episodes. 29.

I
see
you
not

but
I
love
you

I
love

Robert Lax,
December 1993 notebook entry

Sketch by S.T. Georgiou. The author regularly drew this image on correspondence he would send to Robert Lax.

Think of yourself as a traveler, and think of spiritual friends as guides; think of their instructions as the road, and think of the practices as going to the land of your destination. Think of yourself crossing to the other shore, and think of the spiritual friend as boatman; think of the instruction as a ford, and think of the practices as a boat...

"The Sutra Arranged Like a Tree," from *The Teacher–Student Relationship*, by Jamgon Kongtrul the Great, translated by Ron Garry.